Marionette Magic
From Concept to Curtain Call

Marionette Magic
From Concept to Curtain Call

Bruce Taylor, *1960-*

Illustrations by Cathy Stubington and Bruce Taylor

TAB TAB BOOKS Inc.
Blue Ridge Summit, PA

FIRST EDITION
FIRST PRINTING

Copyright © 1989 by Bruce Taylor.
Printed in the United States of America

Library of Congress Cataloging in Publication Data

Taylor, Bruce, 1960-
   Marionette magic : from concept to curtain call / by Bruce Taylor ; illustrations by Cathy Stubington and Bruce Taylor.
     p. cm.
   Includes index.
   Summary: Provides detailed instructions for inventing and constructing string puppets and staging a marionette production.
   ISBN 0-8306-9091-3   ISBN 0-8306-9391-2 (pbk.)
   1. Puppet making.   2. Puppets and puppet-plays.   [1. Puppets.
2. Puppet making.   3. Puppet plays.]   I. Stubington, Cathy, ill.
II. Title.
TT174.7.T39   1988   88-26556
745.592′24—dc19   CIP
                                         AC

TAB BOOKS Inc. offers software for sale. For information and a catalog, please contact TAB Software Department, Blue Ridge Summit, PA 17294-0850.

Questions regarding the content of this book should be addressed to:

   Reader Inquiry Branch
   TAB BOOKS Inc.
   Blue Ridge Summit, PA 17294-0214

Contents

Acknowledgments

Thanks to Leslie Ashton, Peter Duschenes, Jano Salinas, and everyone who has contributed time, effort, and original ideas to the Picardi Marionette Theatre.

Introduction

PUPPETRY IS FOR VISIONARIES WITH HUMBLE MEANS. IN THIS AGE OF SPECIAL-ists, the puppeteer is something of an oddity. While others sell life insurance, yank teeth, and drive forklifts, the puppeteer builds entire worlds. Of course, the world over which the puppeteer presides might be less than 1½ feet wide and as little as 3 feet from one side to the other. The puppets themselves might be patched together from a heap of old newspapers, a bag of rags, and a bundle of sticks.

Although the scenery is diminutive and the actors handmade, there is nothing paltry about the effect a puppet show has upon its audience. A puppet show can be every bit as lofty, funny, touching, sad, or frightening as a legitimate theatrical performance, and because puppets are not inconvenienced by such trifles as the law of gravity, puppetry can create magical effects that could never be brought to a full-sized stage. Thus, puppetry, the humblest of the dramatic arts, is in some ways the most versatile. It allows you to think big on a small scale.

All of these things make the puppet show an ideal form of theatre for the nonprofessional. Not surprisingly, puppetry has always been a popular hobby or avocation. One of the features of puppetry that is most appealing to nonactors is the simple fact that the puppeteers do not need to appear on the stage. They are generally hidden behind a mask, curtain, or screen. This makes puppetry the perfect medium for shy exhibitionists and closet extroverts. No matter how bizarre and overblown the characters they create, the puppeteers themselves remain anonymous and apart.

This is particularly true of the traditional marionette. A string puppet is connected to its manipulator by five or ten fine nylon threads. To the audience, these strings are all but invisible, so the marionette gives the illusion of being a freestanding, independently articulated creature. It seems to be *alive*. With the proper lighting and scenery, the illusion can be quite startling.

This book offers a complete behind-the-backdrops introduction to the world of the traditional jointed wooden string puppet. It was written with three types of readers in mind.

The first kind of readers has a passion for woodworking, but can't face the prospect of another spice rack, spoon rest, or napkin caddy. He is probably intrigued by wooden objects with moving parts, and might have tried his hand at a whirligig or wooden toy. If he has children or gandchildren, he will certainly realize that a well-crafted string puppet makes a superb gift for any child. This reader is interested in learning to build a traditional string puppet, but have no wish (at this point) to put on a whole show. The first six chapters of this book will tell him everything he needs to know about constructing a marionette.

The second kind of reader faces a predicament. He has rashly agreed to prepare an act for the church gala (or the company Christmas show, the lodge fundraiser, the community center charity benefit...whatever). Wisely deciding to mount a puppet spectacle, he procures a copy of this book. It will tell him how to conceive an idea for a show, how to write the script (or get away with *not* writing one), how to make and clothe a full cast of marionettes—in short, everything he needs to know to put on a performance.

Category number three includes readers who have an ongoing interest in puppetry as a dramatic form and wish to develop their skills. Such a reader might be a drama teacher, a student of set design, a professional puppeteer, or simply an interested amateur. For these individuals, this book offers a full apprenticeship in the art of string puppetry.

The final three chapters will be of particular interest to the third category of readers. Chapter VI deals with specialty puppets—weightlifters, disjointing skeletons, and so forth. Chapter VII includes diagrams and specifications for making a portable touring stage. Chapter VIII deals with special effects, revealing how to make a dragon puff smoke, how to set a shockingly realistic stage fire, and how to make objects appear out of, or disappear into, thin air. Some of the techniques I describe are traditional; others are recent inventions. Many have never been described in print.

You don't have to be an experienced woodworker or sculptor to build a functioning marionette. All the procedures described in this book are broken down into simple steps that assume no prior knowledge of puppetry. Throughout, I have stuck to the principle that it is better to provide thorough instructions for one procedure than to give skimpy instructions for two.

I have not attempted to cover every last thing you might want to do on marionette stage. Some puppet books try to be encyclopedic, listing dozens of ways to accomplish a single task—a task that, as often as not, you will never wish to perform anyway. Rather than waste space describing ten ways to make a marionette doff his cap, I supply you with one method that *works*. I have tried to provide a sampling of basic techniques that can be changed or adapted easily. Thus, while your puppet might never need to remove his hat, you can use the remove his sunglasses.

The tools and materials needed to make a marionette are fairly simple and inexpensive. This is not to say that you couldn't spend a lot of money if you tried. Every puppeteer has a dream workshop in his imagination. Mine has vast expanses of countertop and miles of shelving fixed to the walls, on which hundreds of pots of paint and glue are lined up beside trim rows of color-coordinated jars full of nuts and bolts. Where there are no shelves, the walls are covered with fine tools, boxwood mallets, oriental saws, and newly honed chisels arranged in descending order of size. In reality, of course, I am more likely to find myself squatting on the basement floor with two slabs of wood clamped between my toes.

The type of workshop doesn't seem to affect the quality of the finished product. When you don't have the right tool, the wrong tool often will work well enough. Just make sure that the tools you select can do the job *safely*. Don't try driving screws with a bread knife, for instance—at best you will find this difficult; at worst, you will slice off a finger. In some cases a power tool, such as a glue gun or rotary rasp, can save you a lot of trouble. However, any of the projects described in this book can be produced with a modest selection of ordinary hand tools and household materials. At the beginning of each project, I list all the equipment you will require. The lists are never long, and the tools are generally quite ordinary.

I

The Squeaking Tribe

And now the squeaking tribe proceeding roams
O'er painted mansions, and illustrious domes;

. . .

All actions that on life's great stage appear
In miniature are represented here

"A Puppet Show" (1716)
Joseph Addison

PUPPETS ARE FASCINATING, SO YOU MIGHT EXPECT THE HISTORY OF PUPPETRY to be fascinating as well. However, it is not fascinating at all. In fact, for the most part, puppet history is rather dry stuff and for a simple reason: puppetry is a folk art. In the Western world, puppet shows have always been produced by and for the common people, and because a majority of the undertakings of such people usually are not considered worth recording, a great deal has been lost. There are few great events or raging conflicts in the history of puppets. There has been many a Charlemagne puppet, but never a puppet Charlemagne to enliven the story of "the squeaking tribe."

Nevertheless, I feel it is important to give a brief outline of puppetry through the ages, because anybody who wishes to be initiated into this venerable art ought to know a bit about its ancient traditions. If you are interested in knowing the whole story, consult a history of puppetry such as George Speaight's meticulously researched *History of the English Puppet Theatre,* or Paul McPharlin's *The Puppet Theatre in America,* a 700-page book that tells as much about this subject as any person with a normal life span would care to know.

1

everywhere in the world. It is not known where the art began, or why it was first practiced. Some writers propose that the first puppets might have been religious idols with moving parts. Such statues are found in many civilizations. The famous Christ of Boxley, made sometime in the fifteenth century, had the power to move its limbs, roll its eyes, and open its lower lip as if speaking. Cynics might assume such a contraption was used by an enterprising priesthood to mystify and exploit credulous churchgoers. But the truth might be more complicated. It is very common throughout the world for the devout to act out their religious mysteries in semitheatrical ways. Devotees often represent their divinities in masks and cult figures and enact old myths and sacred stories in song and dance. It is a way of attempting to make spiritual events happen in this world, and need not imply fraud. The Boxley Crucifix might well have been used in religious pageants like the passion plays that are still acted out every ten years in the city of Oberammergau.

Another source for the Western puppet theatre might have been classical drama, which itself had religious origins in the festival of the god Dionysus at Athens. Greek actors wore masks and produced sophisticated illusions using elaborate stage machinery. The comedy was ribald and wildly satirical. Clearly, Greek and Roman slapstick had a lot in common with the puppet theatre as we know it today, but it was all done on a rather lavish scale. If there was a separate classical tradition of true puppetry, its memory has not been preserved.

There are no clear references to puppets in ancient Greek or Roman literature, although jointed figurines dating from classical times have been unearthed. These might have had a religious use, or they might have been mere toys. The modeling of the figures is not particularly theatrical, so it seems unlikely that they were brought before the public in any sort of puppet show. Whatever purpose they served, they had metal rods attached to the tops of their heads, as some types of marionettes do to this day. They must have been held by these rods and made to mimic human movements, so it makes some sense to describe them as puppets, as some writers have done (FIG. 1-1).

There are very few references to puppets or puppet shows in the Middle Ages. Parchment was precious and the people who knew how to write had other things to write about. Still, it is clear that hand puppets were common enough in the late Middle Ages and early Renaissance. In 1573, the Lord Mayor of London is recorded as having given permission for a puppet company "to carry on their strange motions as in the past and from time immemorial." The phrase *time immemorial* makes it clear that puppets were no novelty. In this period, traveling shows were the main source of popular entertainment, and troupes of acrobats, jugglers, minstrels, and illusionists would work their way from one town to the next, performing in squares, fairs, marketplaces, aristocrats' houses, and even, if they were particularly fortunate or talented, the royal courts.

The professional puppeteers of this era would have made their living in this way, alongside knife-throwers, bear-baiters, and buffoons. Puppetry, after all, was not a respectable profession. There is no way to glamorize the early years of the traveling hand puppet show. Until well into the nineteenth century, puppetry

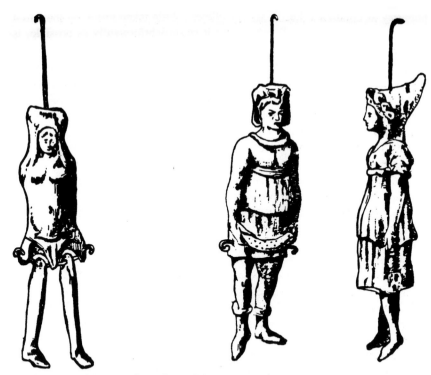

Fig. 1-1. Jointed figurines from classical Greece (left) and Rome (right). From an engraving by Hermann Siegfried Rehm (1905).

offered the same sort of attraction as dancing bears, tumblers, wild men, and five-legged goats. In 1805, the poet Wordsworth published his description of St. Bartholomew's fair, showing the kind of company puppeteers kept:

> All moveables of wonder from all parts
> Are here—Albinos, painted Indians, Dwarfs,
> The Horse of Knowledge, and the learned Pig,
> the Stone-eater, the man that swallows fire,
> Giants, Ventriloquists, the Invisible Girl,
> The bust that speaks and moves its goggling eyes
> the Wax-work, Clock-work, all the marvelous craft
> Of modern Merlins, Wild beasts, Puppet-shows,
> All out-o'-the-way, far-fetched, perverted things.

That puppets should be considered "far-fetched, perverted things" might seem peculiar to a generation weaned on the cuddly monsters of "*Sesame Street*", but the puppet shows of this era featured grotesque parodies of well-known stories, acted out with plenty of indecent jokes, topical satire, and comical violence.

Anyone who has seen an authentic Punch and Judy show will have little trouble imagining the hand puppet theatre of Wordsworth's day. People who think of exposure to a real Punch. Punch, to put it as nicely as possible, is a mass murderer. He torments his dog, drops the baby on its head, and laughs merrily as he clubs one puppet after another until he has beaten them all to death. Punch is physically monstrous, with a huge stomach protruding in front and a massive, sickle-shaped hump rising behind (FIG. 1-2). He is a manic punster and singer of off-color songs; in fact, he jokes and sings even as he is dragged off to be hanged for his crimes.

Fig. 1-2. Punch as etched by George Cruikshank in Punch and Judy *magazine (1873).*

If Punch seems like an unlikely puppet hero, bear in mind that he is a relic of a less squeamish era, harkening back to a time when showmen would release a bull with fireworks strapped to its back and a cat tied to its tail. These days puppeteers are usually quite careful to avoid offending their audience. But Punch is offensive to one and all, which is precisely what has made him the most popular English puppet for the past 300 years (FIG. 1-3).

STRING PUPPETS

The origin of string puppets is as obscure as that of hand puppets. A well-known illustration from a twelfth century manuscript shows two youths amusing themselves with a pair of small figures mounted on horizontal ropes. This seems to have been a kind of game, rather than a true puppet show. All the same, it is the earliest known representation of a string-operated puppet (FIG. 1-4).

4

Fig. 1-3. Punch tossing his own baby off the stage.

Sometime in the mid-seventeenth century we begin to see evidence that string marionette shows were being produced. String puppetry usually requires a more elaborate stage than glove puppets, so it might be that social and economic conditions prevented showmen from putting on marionette shows until this time. In any case, it was not until the eighteenth century that the string puppet really came into its own. About this time showmen in various parts of Europe began to produce elaborate marionette shows exploiting the full range of movements and illusionistic potential of a permanent stage. The jointed wooden string marionette began its long career as the most elegant and versatile of the puppets. The tradition out of which this book is written had its origins during this period.

In the string puppets of the eighteenth century, we can see virtually all the main features of the marionette theatre as it is known today. Characters and techniques that are still in use had their origins in the marionette theatres of that

5

Fig. 1-4. Two youths playing a game with puppets. After illustrations in the manuscript Hortus Deliciarum *(1170).*

era. Some puppets, such as the famous "dissecting skeleton," have survived virtually unchanged, and are as appealing today as they were 200 years ago.

The earliest string puppets were quite small and had thin metal rods attached to the tops of their heads. The rigidity of the rods made it easy for manipulators to maintain complete control over the puppet. The heads and trunks of the puppets could be turned swiftly and with some accuracy, making this a relatively versatile style of puppet. It remained popular for several hundred years, and is still common in many parts of the Old World. Unfortunately, the metal rods attached to the puppets heads make the puppets move as if they had metal rods attached to their heads. They impose a stiff, vertical posture, making it difficult for the puppeteer to mimic the fluid and supple movements of the human body. Also, the relatively thick rods are difficult to conceal from the audience.

The rod became a major limitation as puppeteers became more adept, attempting ever more ambitious deceptions. At some point somebody had the idea of replacing the rod with two or more strings. The connection between puppet and manipulator dwindled to a thread, and the modern marionette was born (FIG. 1-5).

6

Fig. 1-5. An early representation of Punch as a string puppet. The other puppet might be Joan (later known as Judy). This Punch and the elaborate stage he is standing on belonged to the most famous ''puppet-show-man'' of the eighteenth century: Robert Powell. Powell, who was not much taller than a puppet himself, was said to have earned ''such wealth as is sufficient to buy all the poets in England.'' From A Second Tale of a Tub *(1715).*

By the mid-1800s, all-string puppets had become remarkably popular. Marionettes naturally lent themselves to lavish display of scenery and special effects. Puppet showmen were not slow to take advantage of the string puppet's superior mobility.

A hand puppet fits like a glove over the puppeteer's fingers, and therefore can't go anywhere without taking the puppeteer with him. As a result, there are some things the glove puppet simply can't do. He can't perform a somersault, for example, unless the puppeteer somersaults with him, and he can never fly through the air. The wooden string puppet, however, is manipulated from a distance by means of nearly invisible threads, and can be made to perform all sorts of difficult maneuvers. In the earliest days of the marionette theatre, this ability encouraged showmen to incorporate trick puppets and specialty routines into their acts.

Just as the first filmmakers were often infatuated with special effects, reveling in the illusionistic power of their new medium, the string puppeteers of the nineteenth century began to build whole shows around mechanical tricks, scenic effects, and mysterious transformations. These trick marionettes were often billed as "fantoccini," borrowing the Italian name for this type of puppet. Fantoccini variety shows became extremely common in the second half of the century. One of the best-known troupes was W. J. Bullock's Royal Marionettes, which astonished the public with pole balancers; tightrope walkers; bottle jugglers; a four-headed, neck-stretching Scaramouche; and the always popular dissecting skeleton. With life-sized puppets and a 20-piece band, this kind of event had more in common with music hall comedy or stage conjuring than with the poor traveling Punch and Judy plays.

The fantoccini continued to be immensely popular for at least two decades, attracting large paying audiences throughout Europe and North America until the turn of the century. Then, without warning, calamity struck in the form of the motion picture show. The cinema offered a world of illusions far richer than that of the string puppets. The little jugglers and neck stretchers could not compete, and the string marionette faded into near oblivion.

Perhaps public interest would not have collapsed so abruptly if only the marionette showmen had continued to develop puppetry as drama, entertaining people with lively characterization and storytelling, instead of dazzling them with special effects. In any case, the jointed wooden string puppet went into an eclipse that lasted about three decades. When the art began to be revived in the 1930s, it was not the novelty aspect of the puppets that interested showpeople but the potential for dramatic expression.

As writers and journalists have often noted, usually with surprise, puppet shows can be every bit as elegant, powerful, or touching as the legitimate theatre. Puppetry has a distinctive character and charm, which set it apart from the other theatrical arts. A marionette is not just a second-rate copy of a live person. An unmoving mask can be as poignant, piercing, or expressive as any grimacing Olivier or scowling Brando; and the stiff tentative movements of a wooden marionette can be as heartrending or hilarious as the occasion requires. The poet

Arthur Symons, writing in 1902, argues that puppets were not only equal to live actors, but superior. Living actors, he says, always permit their own temperaments and personalities to intrude upon the scenes, whereas the puppet actor is never out of character. In other words, if you can't afford to hire a Sir John Gielgud, then build one of your own.

With that fine sentiment, we proceed to the next chapter, where you will begin making your marionette. You will start at the top, plunging into puppetry "head first."

II

Heads

The artist's skill contrives the wooden race
And carves in lifeless sticks the human face;
Then shapes the trunk and then the parts assigns
And limbs to limbs in meet proportions joins.

"A Puppet Show" (1716)
Joseph Addison

WHO IS THIS MARIONETTE YOU'RE ABOUT TO BUILD? AS A PUPPETEER-TO-BE, YOU must start thinking about your marionette as if it were alive, and you must regard yourself, in all humility, as a creator of life. The most important question as you set to work is not "What will it be made of?" but, "Who will it be?" I might have begun this chapter with a description of methods, materials, and techniques, but instead I'll start by discussing *characters*. Without a character, a puppet is nothing but a doll.

CHARACTERS

For many thousands of years, it has been considered a matter of plain, good sense to judge a person's character by the appearance of his face. At one time, the practice was even made scientifically respectable in the lofty and dignified "science" of *physiognomy*, the study of the human face. Until the late nineteenth century, physiognomists were as common as diet doctors are today. They found an eager and credulous public for their ideas, which they popularized in thick, luxuriously illustrated volumes, arguing that people's facial features revealed their

... ...litics. Thick line was a sign of indolence; a sharp nose indicated
wart on her chin, she could at least claim to be prudent and hard-working. It was as straightforward as arithmetic (FIG. 2-1).

Fig. 2-1. An illustration from Johann Caspar Lavater's Physiognomy (1750), showing "a countenance by vice rendered fiend-like, abhorrent to nature, in which fallaciousness is sunken almost below bestiality."

In our time, this "science of human nature" has been discredited, and physiognomy is a curiosity of the past—except, that is, in the puppet world. Somehow, the scientific revolutions that have rocked the twentieth century have passed the puppets by, and among the marionettes, physiognomy lives on. Beady eyes still connote criminality; a big chin is heroic; drooping eyelids hint that a character is slow-witted, and a slack jaw confirms it. There's an old saying: "It is not the beard that makes the philosopher." But puppetry turns that platitude upside down. As a puppeteer, you can put a beard on a stale bun or a brown paper bag and make a perfectly believable philosopher. In puppetry, appearances are *not* deceiving, all that glitters *is* gold, and you *can* judge a book by its cover. If a character looks rotten, he simply is.

There are hundreds of stock character traits available to the puppeteer. Cartoonists use them all the time, identifying a pirate with a black eyepatch or a drunkard with a red nose. The marionette maker should have some understanding of these conventions. This doesn't mean he should follow them blindly—there's a fine line between drawing on a tradition and rehashing a cliché. But if his puppets' faces are to be interpreted correctly, the craftsman must understand his audience's preconceptions and take them into account. It's just good showmanship.

Some people assume that puppet physiognomy is an inflexible code, and that there are simple "recipes" for character types. To cook up a "cute" character, you just give it a chubby, round face, a high forehead, and wide eyes. To make a villain, start with an oval head, give it arched, downswept eyebrows and a nose like a buzzard's beak, and set the whole thing off with a sneaky grin (FIG. 2-2). These kinds of guidelines are useful for making immediately recognizable stock characters, but keep in mind that it's very hard to concoct a full and interesting character from a jumble of stereotypes. What's more, it's possible to flout *all* the rules and still come up with a character that's exactly right.

In recent years, the movie industry has made a cuddly screen hero out of a bug-eyed, hose-necked, baggy-skinned extraterrestrial, so you actually have a lot of leeway. You should definitely experiment with new ways of representing common character types. Of course, if you decide to make your Prince Charming a beady-eyed, pointy-nosed hunchback, you really have your work cut out for you! You'll have to contend with every cleft chin and pageboy haircut your

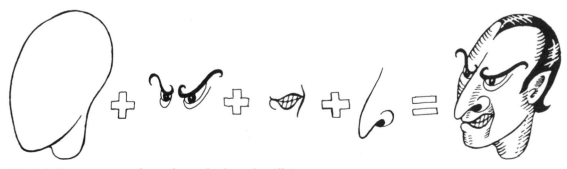

Fig. 2-2. The components that make up the face of a villain.

Marionette theatre, like any other kind of theatre, plays games with the audience's expectations, either fulfilling them or overturning them. Even when he is building his actors, the puppeteer is already playing to an audience—in his own mind at least. He is doing with wood or papier-mâché exactly what an actor does with his own face: creating a character. So think of yourself as an actor and get into a role. (That's something ordinary woodworkers never get to do.) Stare at yourself in the mirror and practice the facial expressions you will give your puppet. Make faces while you're making faces! The more fun you have, the more lively the finished marionette will be.

By now it should be clear that a character is an individual being, not a facial or racial "type." Over the years, many puppeteers have failed to make the distinction. "Chinese" is not a character. "Crippled" is not a character. These are features which a character may possess, but if you give your puppet no individual qualities except "chineseness" or "crippledness," the results will be at best uninteresting, and at worst extremely offensive.

FINDING YOUR CHARACTER

The first thing you must realize is that a puppet is not a creature of this world. He is a citizen of the imagination. He lives in response to the characters and events of a story. Your understanding of his personality begins in the world of his story. You must discover your character in the imaginary facts of his imaginary life.

Chances are you'll work from a story that already exists. It's possible to invent an engaging character and build the story around him or her, but for now let's assume you've selected a story. You've thought about it a lot, and you've gotten to the point where you feel you know the characters. They've begun to come alive for you.

Let's say your story has an old king in it who is cruel to his only son. Ask yourself why he acts this way. It could be several things. Maybe he's basically a good man, but rather weak and silly. He permits himself to be manipulated by a treacherous advisor; the advisor has designs on the throne and therefore wants the son out of the way. One way to underscore the king's weakness would be to make him look feeble and tired. Perhaps he's happy to be deceived, as long as nobody interferes with his sleep. If so, you might give him a soft, doughy face, sagging eyes, a pillowy white beard and a vague mouth. As you visualize this character you should be asking questions about him. Has he always been slightly daft? Or is he a strong, sensible ruler who has gone to seed? Will he eventually snap out of his lethargy, or is he a lost cause?

Then suppose he's an altogether different sort of creature, one who is not vague and sleepy, but paranoid and suspicious. He is possessed by an unreasoning fear that his son will try to depose him. This makes him aggressive, capricious, and prone to fits of rage. You might want to make him wild and furious-looking. Give him narrowed eyes and firey brows. Give him a forked beard, a mouth

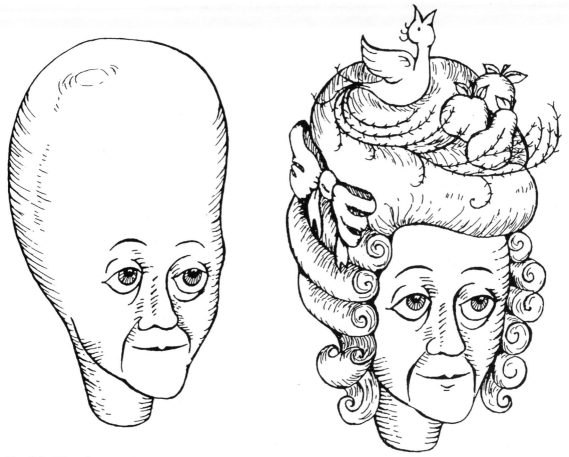

Fig. 2-3. When designing heads, you can mold or carve the hair, moustache, or beard directly onto the head itself. If the puppet is to have a strange hat or fancy hairstyle, you can sculpt a basic form and then paint or decorate it later.

clenched in a perpetual grimace, unruly hair and a bright red complexion. Now reconsider. Is there a better way to see this character?

When you're satisfied with your answers to these questions, you're ready to sit down and sketch a portrait of your king. This stage isn't absolutely necessary. If you'd rather start your puppet right away, go ahead. However chances are you'll find it useful to have a rough drawing to work from (FIG. 2-3).

Take a few sheets of unlined, white paper and use any drawing implement that you're comfortable with. (I prefer a black felt-tipped pen, because when I use a pencil I get obsessive about erasing and correcting and don't spend enough time experimenting.) Let your imagination loose, and while you're sketching heads I have a few things to say about *style*.

STYLE

It is style that unifies and connects the puppets in a show, however different they are in character and appearance. Your puppet heads should seem to belong together, like the pieces in a chess set. In a set of chess pieces, the king, the bish-op, and the pawns are all very different in size and shape, but together they must form a connected series. The pieces from a carved Mexican alabaster chess set will look inappropriate if mixed in with those of a lathed wooden set. Some sets are simple and abstract; others are detailed and realistic. It's a matter of style (FIG. 2-4).

A consistent visual style is usually (in this book I'll try to avoid saying "always") highly desirable. When many people are working together on the same show, it's best if one person designs—and, if possible, sculpts—all of the heads. If several people share this job, then several styles will share the stage. In this case, one head is better than two.

Once you've found an appropriate style, a lot of other things will fall into place. There are several ways to go about it. First of all, it can't be stressed too strongly that there's no such thing as "The Marionette Style". Marionettes don't have to look like the marionettes you've already seen, nor should they. There have been cubist and surrealist marionette shows, shows that accurately recreate a historical period, and shows that used puppets made out of kitchen utensils. So there's no need to hitch yourself to a style you're not comfortable with. You'll probably find that you have a natural style that makes anything you draw or sculpt distinctly and uniquely yours if you just do what comes naturally.

On the other hand, you could be more deliberate about it and adapt some existing style to the puppet stage. If you want to do a play set in ancient Egypt, for instance, you might base your style on Egyptian frescoes and sculptures. If you're adapting a Viking myth, you could look at Norse wood and stone carvings. It's mostly a question of taste.

You might favor a simple geometrical style, or you might go in for an ornate Gothic style. You might want your puppets to look pale, elongated, and ethereal, or you might like them stout and stumpy. Follow your inclinations—there's no "right" way to design a puppet. The only limitation is that it must be mechanically functional. We'll discuss that side of things presently (FIG. 2-5).

If you have trouble thinking up faces for your characters, you might consider basing them on paintings or on illustrations from a book. This is an excellent way to get ideas, but be aware that a painting is static and two-dimensional, while a marionette must come to life on the stage. As a general rule, a marionette's face should be somewhat exaggerated so that it can be "read" from a distance. And, needless to say, if you give your puppet an angry face, be sure that he doesn't have to act jolly at some point in the show.

MAKING THE HEAD

A marionette head can be carved out of Styrofoam, modeled in paste, or cut out of a plastic bottle. It can be cast in latex rubber, molded from sawdust and glue, or even twisted in wire. However, this book is about the traditional marionette, so we will concentrate on the traditional materials: wood, plaster, and papier-mâché. Of these media the most versatile, rugged, and easy to master is papier-mâché. We'll touch briefly on plaster and wood, and then move on to what I consider the best procedure for making heads.

16

Fig. 2-4. Separately, these two puppets would be quite nice, but together they look ridiculous because they are stylistically incompatible.

Fig. 2-5. A gallery of puppet heads in different styles.

Plaster

A very nice puppet head can be made out of plaster, and the process is an easy one. However, the finished head will be difficult to repair when it breaks—and it *will* break sooner or later, because plaster is brittle, puppeteers are careless, and kids will be kids. Plaster is also quite heavy, so if it falls your puppet will probably crack its own skull, and you'll spend many unhappy hours getting your head together.

On the other hand, you might like the method for making plaster heads. The technique involves a mixture of modeling and carving. First you model a crude shape from a blob of very thick plaster, then you refine the form with a penknife and some sandpaper. It's not too difficult. Plaster is a relatively forgiving medium for inexperienced sculptors: it's soft enough to be carved with household tools, and if, in your creative frenzy, you amputate your puppet's chin, it's possible to fashion a new one in a matter of minutes (provided the head has not yet been painted).

If you feel comfortable with plaster and can live with its limitations, proceed as follows.

> **Tools and Materials**
>
> - Penknife.
> - Plaster of Paris.
> - Sandpaper.
> - Tea sieve.
> - Mixing bowl.
> - Rasp.

1. Place ¼ cup of water in a shallow mixing bowl. Add plaster slowly, sifting it through a tea sieve and stirring constantly. When the mixture becomes too thick to stir, knead it with your free hand. Keep this up until the plaster reaches the consistency of a thick dough. Make sure there are no pockets of dry plaster; if necessary, add more water.

2. Plaster, you will quickly discover, is not an ideal modeling medium. If you attempt to mold subtle and complex forms your efforts will end in exasperation. At this stage you should concentrate on making a rudimentary shape, suitable for carving. The material will start to set shortly after you begin working with it, and if you tamper with the plaster while it is setting, you'll weaken the final product. Work fast and don't fuss over your creation, even if it looks like something that crawled out of a chemical waste dump (FIG. 2-6).

3. When it has set, take a fairly rugged knife with a short, not-too-sharp blade and start blocking out the most prominent features—usually the nose, chin, and cheekbones. Proceed carefully: it's easier to carve plaster than to uncarve it. Fine details—lines around the eyes, and so on—can be etched in with carving tools. Use a rasp to grind down any lumps and bulges. Smooth with sandpaper (FIG. 2-7).

Fig. 2-6. *The humble beginnings of a plaster head.*

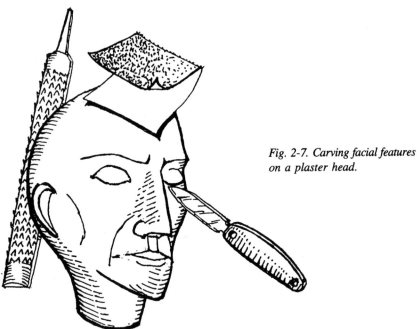

Fig. 2-7. *Carving facial features on a plaster head.*

4. If you chop off some important feature by mistake you can repair the damage with fresh plaster. First, though, to make the plaster stick, you must gouge a hole in the puppet's face, just as a dentist drills a tooth before inserting the filling. Hopefully this won't be necessary, but if it is, refer to FIG. 2-8.

5. When it comes time to paint the head, use a thick enamel or give it at least one coat of a heavy varnish, such as Varethane Liquid Plastic. This keeps moisture out and adds a bit of strength to the surface.

20

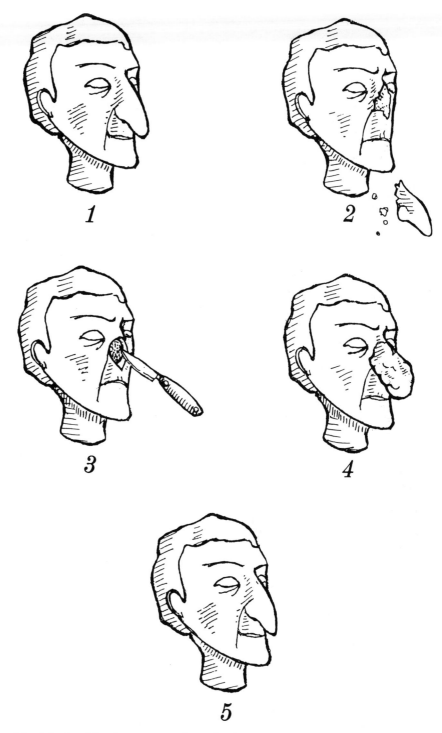

Fig. 2-8. Repairing damage to a plaster head.

Wood

Pinocchio had a wooden head. Carlo Collodi's classic story has fixed forever in the public mind the image of Geppetto, the loving craftsman, brushing wood shavings from the face of a little wooden boy. And to this day, many people think wood is the only suitable material for a puppet's noggin.

A wooden head has many advantages (on a puppet, that is). Wood, depending on the kind you use, can be a very durable material—though, like plaster, it is difficult to mend when it breaks. A skilled carver can achieve very delicate effects. For fine lines and detailed work, wood has a slight edge over papier-mâché. And there's something indefinably *right* about wood. It's like having real plants in your fishtank. Eventually the wood will be covered up, but it's still a pleasure just to know it's there, under the paint.

However, all of this means nothing if you don't know how to carve. And that's the main drawback. No matter how you slice, chop, or chisel it, wood is a relatively resistant material. You can't just dig into a hunk of mahogany with a kitchen knife (as you can a block of plaster, for instance). Learning to carve the face of your dreams could keep you so busy that you never get around to building the rest of your puppet. But, of course, this might suit your interests perfectly. If you have the tools, inclination, and aptitude for carving, I suggest you proceed as follows.

Tools and Materials

- Block of pine, basswood, poplar, willow, mahogany, birch, or maple.
- Soft lead pencil.
- Coping saw (or scroll saw, if available).
- Jackknife.
- Vise.
- Woodcarving tools: chisel, extra-flat gouge, deep gouge, V-tool.
- Mallet.
- Rasp.

---

1. Start with a block of wood slightly larger than the head you envision (taking the neck into account). If you're an experienced carver, you might choose a fine-grained hardwood such as maple, birch, or mahogany. Otherwise, pine, poplar, basswood, or willow are best. Make sure the pieces you select are free of knots and cracks, and that the grain runs vertically, from scalp to chin.

2. Draw the front view and profile of your character on the block using a soft pencil (FIG. 2-9).

3. Cut out the rough shape with a saw. If you have the use of a band saw or scroll saw, count yourself lucky—it will make the job a lot easier. Otherwise, struggle along with a coping saw. Use a vise! Your left hand is a poor substitute, and there's no substitute for a lopped-off thumb (FIG. 2-10).

22

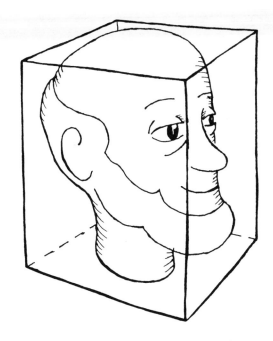

Fig. 2-9. Draw the outline for a wooden head.

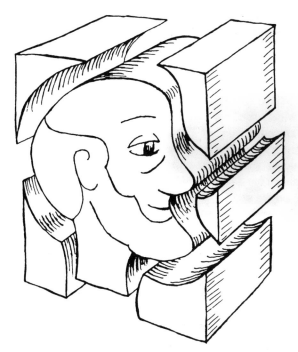

Fig. 2-10. Cut out the basic shape of a wooden head.

4. You might be able to cut the nose with a saw, depending on the shape of the face you are making. In any case, be careful not to cut too deeply, or your puppet's cheeks will have a deflated look. The human nose usually meets the cheeks in a gentle slope. If you slice too far in you will create a nose that juts right out, and your Queen of the Fairies will look like a robot.

5. When you've cut away as much superfluous wood as you can remove with a saw, start rounding out the shape, removing corners, and blocking out the large facial features (nose, chin, cheekbones, eye sockets). This work, which woodworkers call "boasting in" or "roughing in," can be done well with a flat chisel, an extra-flat gouge or even, if the wood is fairly soft, a strong jackknife. You might be surprised at how much of this work can be done with a rasp. A hardware store can sell you a rotary rasp attachment for an electric drill (FIG. 2-11). They are a lot better than ordinary rasps for roughing out concave surfaces.

If you want to make things even easier on yourself, you can buy a special hand-held electric grinding tool. One of these can be fitted with a wide assortment of attachments including rasps, files, sanding drums, and tiny saws. If you can afford one, hesitate no longer. Rotary power tools are useful for making puppet bodies as well. If you invest in one you may find yourself doing much of your carving with it.

6. At this point, when you have the nose, chin, and cheeks roughed out, you might wish to stop carving and finish the surface. Eyes, lips, and other details can be painted on later. If you want to carve these features into the wood itself, now is the time to get out your fine chisels, V-tools, and deep gouges. Again, if the wood is fairly soft you can get away with a jackknife.

Working with Balsa Wood

I've made it sound as if all woods are hard to work with, but of course this is not the case. It's possible to whittle very satisfactory faces out of balsa wood, using simple tools. Balsa, which is widely used for building scale models and miniatures, has properties unlike any other wood. It's very soft and light, and compared to other woods, very fragile. Blocks of the stuff are usually available at hobby and art supply stores. The chief disadvantage of balsa, aside from its weakness, is that it has a fairly coarse, fibrous grain. This makes it hard to carve smooth, curved surfaces and fine details, but this might be a blessing in disguise, since detailed work is often wasted in a puppet show anyway. You can spend hours refining subtle effects, trying to get the lines around the eyes just so, only to discover that, under the stage lights, the results of your work are invisible at ten paces. So you might actually benefit from a medium that discourages obsessive attention to detail. As a rule, you should aim for broad dramatic effects; at a distance your precious touches will melt into a bleary smudge.

Papier-Mâché

I'll make no attempt to conceal my passion for papier-mâché. I couldn't if I tried. It's strong, light, inexpensive, accessible, durable, and easy to use. In short, it's

Fig. 2-11. Rasp attachments for an electric drill.

the consummate medium for a folk art like puppetry. With nothing more sophisticated than a stack of old newspapers and a mixture of flour and water, you can give substance to your most exotic fancy.

Papier-mâché (French for "mashed paper") has been around almost as long as paper itself: about 18 centuries. Like so many other great ideas, papier-mâché was commonplace in the Orient for a long time before it caught on in the backward West. Shortly after Europeans finally got the hang of paper, they learned how to mix it with paste and recast it in various shapes. Papier-mâché enjoyed a real vogue in seventeenth century France, where it was used for making decorative trays, boxes, and other dainty objects. In a world without plastics, it was soon cultivated as an industrial process for mass-producing jewelry chests, doll heads, and even furniture.

The chief beauty of papier-mâché is that everybody has access to an unlimited supply of its main constituent: newspaper. An issue of the *New York Times* contains the makings of a dozen medium-sized puppet heads.

Certainly it is the most accessible of media, but the virtues of papier-mâché don't end there. Papier-mâché objects can be as light or as heavy as you wish, and pound for pound, papier-mâché is the most resilient of modeling materials. A well-made papier-mâché object can be nearly as tough as a wooden one, and for some purposes, even tougher. It is slightly flexible, so a fall that might knock the nose off of a wooden puppet will cause only superficial damage to a papier-mâché head. (Of course, being hollow, a papier-mâché head is more likely to be crushed if sat on.)

Best of all, papier-mâché is *easy*. I predict that some readers won't believe me, and for that I'll blame their third grade art teachers. Many people continue to think of papier-mâché as something that never worked for them in elementary school. They remember wallowing in paste, with clots of ripped-up paper clinging to everything except their sculpture.

I recall spending many a miserable hour in the art room applying wads of slimy paper to the face of a puppet I was making. Every time I pushed the nose into place it would come off in my hand. Meanwhile my puppet's skull continually changed shape, first bulging out in the middle, then caving in at the sides. I'd been struggling for something like classical beauty, but the result was medieval grotesque, with a face right out of my nastiest nightmare. Papier-mâché, I concluded, was a hoax.

But now I'd like to set the record straight. Papier-mâché, when it is used correctly, is easy and foolproof.

There are two procedures for making heads out of papier-mâché. The first process is the simpler of the two. The second method, which involves pressing the papier-mâché into a plaster mold, allows you to issue extra copies of the same head. Both procedures will enable you to make heads in any size or shape.

Tools and Materials:

- Two or three pounds of fresh plasticine, beige or cream-colored, if possible. (Pale, muted colors will show the shadows well.)
- Pastry flour or household white glue. (You can make all sorts of fancy preparations to use as papier-mâché paste, but for most purposes a mixture of white flour and water will do. The main disadvantage of flour paste is that objects made with it might not fare well in storage. Mice and mites could be attracted to your heads, and if they get wet they might never fully recover, although these problems should not appear if the heads are properly painted and varnished. White glue thinned with water makes a slightly stronger and decidedly more waterproof adhesive.)
- Various modeling tools. (You can buy these or improvise your own from household junk: coffee spoons, ice picks, knitting needles, plastic knives, etc.)
- Vaseline. (Vegetable oil will do in a pinch.)
- Newspaper. (Many types of paper are suitable for papier-mâché, and each has its own properties. Tissue paper will give a very fine, smooth surface. Paper towel has a more rugged texture. Toilet paper can be mushed up and used as a sort of modeling medium, to build up raised surfaces. But the all-purpose paper, suitable for nearly any job, is newsprint.)

---

1. To soften a large lump of cold plasticine you will have to work it between your hands. For this you will need the strength of King Kong. To ease the process, break the plasticine into coin-sized pieces that you can flatten between your fingers. Apply these to the head one by one, building up the shape gradually. You'll find this a lot easier than trying to impose a face on the inchoate mass. The armature in the following diagram is just a strong stick of dowel jammed into a hunk of plasticine (FIG. 2-12).

2. Now is the time to play around. With plasticine you have unlimited freedom. The material is not about to dry up, so you can take as much time as you need. Not satisfied with the nose? Tear it off and make another. The eyes bulge out? Push them in. The mouth looks wrong, but you're not sure how to fix it? Shove it around randomly until you begin to detect that missing quality.

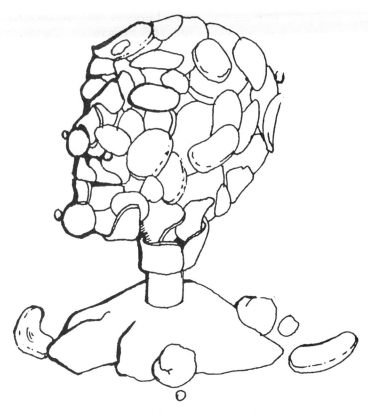

Fig. 2-12. Make the form of a head from pieces of plasticine.

Sometimes you won't know what you're after until you start sculpting. Stay loose and you'll discover new things about your character. Even if you begin with no doubts about how he or she should look, be ready for surprises.

3.   There's something addictive about plasticine, and you might be tempted to prolong the second stage indefinitely. But sooner or later you'll be ready to give your work its permanent form. Mix up a bowl of paste. If you are using flour and water, combine them to the consistency of a thick milkshake. If you're using white glue and water, mix to the consistency of a thin milkshake.

4.   Smear a thin coating of Vaseline over the entire surface of your puppet's face. This is so that the papier-mache won't adhere to the plasticine when it has dried. Make sure that all deep lines and crevices are well coated.

5.   If your puppet face has a lot of detail on it, you might want to use tissue paper for the first layers. Otherwise, take your newsprint and begin ripping it into small pieces. (Don't use scissors to cut the paper. The more ragged the scraps are, the more perfectly their edges will blend in with one another to form a smooth skin). Dip the pieces in your paste and apply them one by one to the surface of the plasticine. On open, flat areas, such as the forehead or cheeks, use pieces about ¾ inch square. Wherever there is a complicated surface to cover—around

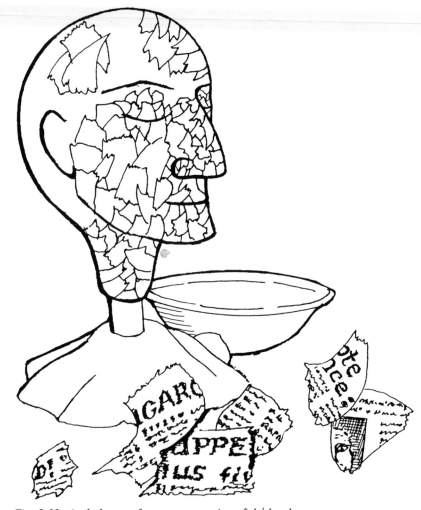

Fig. 2-13. Apply layers of paper on a papier-mâché head.

the eyes, lips or nostrils, for example—you'll have to use smaller scraps. In some places you may need pieces less than an ⅛ inch in length (FIG. 2-13).

Apply three layers of paper, taking care not to distort the original. If you're using tissue paper, lay down four coats. To keep track of how many layers you've applied at any given spot, alternate between two colors of tissue paper. When the head is fully covered, leave it to dry in a warm place for about 12 hours.

6. When the papier-mâché is thoroughly dry, you must cut it in two. Don't be alarmed, it's a routine operation. Take a razor knife or some other sharp implement, steel your nerve and slice the head transversally into two parts. Your cut should pass right through the neck (FIG. 2-14).

7. Now, gently dislodge the plasticine from each half. If you're lucky the plasticine will come away in a lump and your original will be preserved intact. Otherwise you'll have to gouge it out with screwdrivers, nail files, and grape-

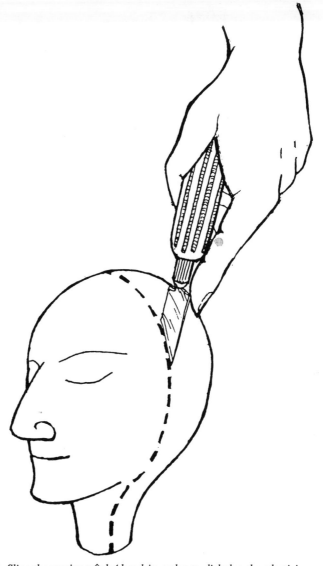

Fig. 2-14. Slice the papier-mâché head in order to dislodge the plasticine.

fruit spoons, or whatever is at hand. Take care. There are only three layers of papier-mâché on the outside surface, so be patient and meticulous. If you lose your head you could lose your head, so to speak (FIG. 2-15).

8.   You now have two rather flimsy papier-mâché shells, corresponding to the front and the back of the head. Mix up another batch of paste and start reinforcing these on the inner surface with more papier-mâché. You should put on another three or four layers before putting the shells aside to dry. As you work, do everything in your power to avoid altering the shape of your two shells. If they sag or twist as they dry the halves won't fit together properly. No matter

Fig. 2-15. The papier-mâché original.

how careful you are, there will be *some* distortion. If you keep it within ³⁄₁₆ inch each way, it shouldn't pose any problems (FIG. 2-16).

9.   When the two parts are dry, prepare one more bowl of paste and patch the halves of the head together. The papier-mâché will be slightly flexible, so it will not be too difficult to disguise all traces of a seam. When the head has dried, it is finished and ready for painting.

Method # 1 works perfectly if your heads are fairly simple. But if a head has a lot of detail it will be very difficult to remain faithful to the plasticine original while you're applying the papier-mâché. In such a case you are better off casting the papier-mâché in a plaster mold, which is Method # 2. This has the added advantage of allowing you to clone your creation, generating any number of identical replicas. It's useful to have more than one of the same head, in case a puppet needs an understudy to stand in for him. For example, suppose your marionette has to change his clothes during the show. In most cases the puppet's strings will pass through holes in his clothing, so undressing a marionette in mid performance is no paltry accomplishment. It's much simpler to have a puppet double on hand. A spare head can also be attached to a special marionette body to make a "stunt puppet," adept at somersaults or dancing.

There is one limitation to plaster casting: there can be no "undercuts" on the face to be cast, or else it will be impossible to remove the papier-mâché from

30

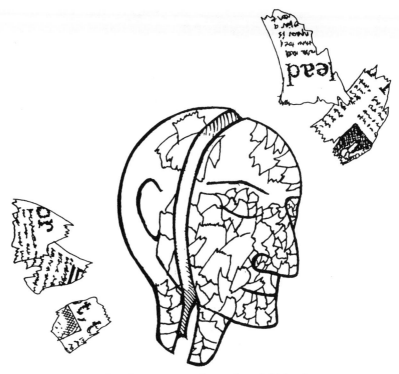

Fig. 2-16. Attach together the two parts of a papier-mâché head.

the mold after it has dried. FIGURE 2-17 shows a puppet that would be very hard to cast in plaster. Actually, this face *could* be cast from a plaster mould, but the two halves of the mold must be made from the sides of the head, rather than the front and the back. Patching the halves together afterward would be somewhat tricky. If you don't follow the reasoning here, read on and it will be clear to you very soon.

The procedure for casting papier-mâché in plaster begins, as the previous method does, with a plasticine sculpture. When you have your plasticine original, proceed as follows.

> **Tools and Materials: Method #2**
> - Wax paper.
> - Tissue paper.
> - A small box.
> - Tea sieve.
> - Plaster of paris.
> - Thread or fine wire.
> - Flour or white glue paste.
> - Vaseline.

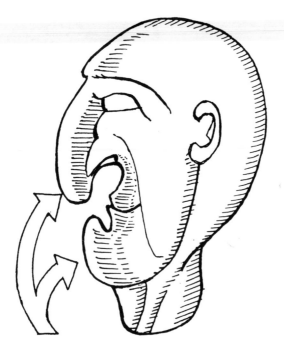

Fig. 2-17. A puppet head that would be difficult to cast in plaster.

1.   If you have not already done so, remove the head from its armature, and plug the neck hole with more plasticine.

2.   Now slice the head transversally into two parts. You can do this with a very thin-bladed knife, but you'll get better results if you use a length of fine, uninsulated wire or fine thread. Stretch the wire or thread between your two hands and draw it through the head (FIG. 2-18).

3.   Smear a thin coating of Vaseline over the entire surface of the puppet's head.

4.   Take a shoe box, or a box of similar size, and line it with wax paper. This gives you a fairly watertight container. Place the two halves of your head (flat side down) in this box (FIG. 2-19).

5.   Prepare a batch of plaster of paris. It's a good idea to sift the plaster through a tea sieve as you stir it into the water, to prevent lumps. Mix the plaster to the consistency of whipping cream.

6.   Pour the plaster into the box. Cover the heads completely, making sure that the highest parts are at least half an inch under the surface of the liquid plaster.

7.   When the plaster has set (allow 2 hours), turn the block over and remove the plasticine. If it was properly coated with Vaseline, you should have no trouble extracting it. If necessary, clean out remaining scraps of plasticine with a toothpick.

8.   You now have two "inside-out" molds of the front and back of the puppet head. Give them a good slathering of Vaseline (FIG. 2-20).

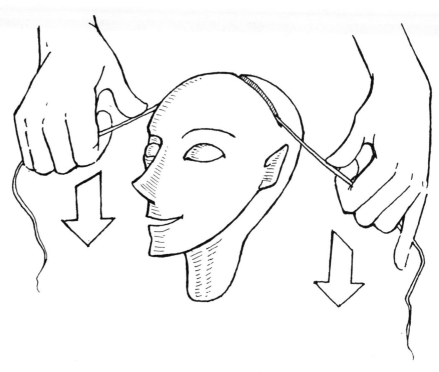

Fig. 2-18. Slice the plasticine form with a heavy thread.

9. Mix a batch of papier-mâché paste, as in the previous method, and cover the inside of the molds with three or four layers of papier-mâché. It's a very good idea to use tissue paper rather than newsprint, because it is finer and will take to the mold more readily. Use very small scraps and press them firmly into all the nooks and cracks.

10. When the papier-mâché is dry, remove the two halves of the head, reinforce the two shells in the inside and reconstruct the head, exactly as in the Method # 1, stages 8 and 9.

PAINTING THE HEAD

No matter what your heads are made of, they will have to be painted. This is not an insignificant part of the process. In fact, in some ways it is the most important. Clever painting can put a convincing face on virtually any surface (FIG. 2-21). Even if your carved head is as plain as an egg you can create a wide range of character traits and expression with nothing but paint. At this stage it's too late to give your puppet a bigger nose, but a good paint job can make the nose he has seem more impressive. Coloring allows you to correct (or create) irregularities in the "skin," and compensate for (or emphasize) any assymetry in the puppet's features.

Stage actors—the flesh and blood kind—have to apply makeup before each performance. Puppets are more fortunate; their makeup is an irremovable fact.

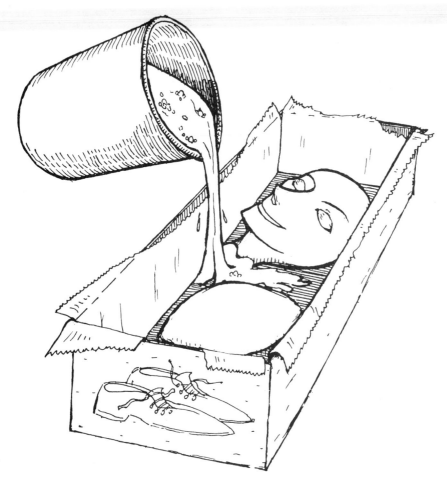

Fig. 2-19. Use a shoe box for pouring plaster.

But the objective is the same: to create fleshtones that look right under the stage lights, and to accentuate character traits.

Colors change under bright overhead lighting, and the kinds of changes that occur will depend on the mix of colors in your stage lights. In general, however, you can expect that most colors will fade, and color contrasts will become less pronounced, so you must adjust the color of your puppets' faces accordingly. In this discussion I'll assume you're striving for natural, realistic fleshtones that will look good on a stage. If you want to make marionettes with lime green faces, or marionettes that will never be in a show, you'll have to adapt these guidelines.

There should be plenty of red in your skin tones, especially in Caucasian characters, because reds and oranges tend to fade more than blues and greens. Different characters will need different fleshtones. For instance, an old character will have more grey in this skin than a young one. But you should not mix up a separate batch of paint for each head. It is best to start with a "base" color,

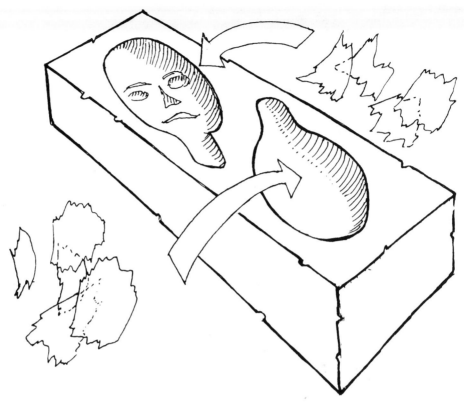

Fig. 2-20. Finished molds for puppet heads.

and adjust the hue and shade for each puppet (and for different areas on the same puppet). This way there will be an underlying continuity in the fleshtones.

Wrinkles and crevices will tend to disappear on stage unless you darken them. If you've ever applied makeup to your own face you know the rule: dark shades recede, light shades come forward. To make hollow cheeks look even hollower, give them a deep, greyish tint. To make the bridge of the nose stand out, trace it with a pale fleshtone.

Almost any type of paint is suitable for painting the heads. I prefer acrylic paint because it is water-soluble, dries quickly, and can be applied either opaquely or as a semitransparent wash. Gouache and poster paint are also excellent. (It doesn't matter if the paint is not waterproof because the heads will be varnished afterwards). Enamel and oil paints dry slowly and require special thinners, most of which are smelly and poisonous. Save yourself the bother.

1. Prime the surface of the head by brushing on a layer of "gesso," a compound used to prepare surfaces for painting. It is available at any art supply store. If you don't feel like paying art store prices for a can of gesso, obtain a small can of white latex paint and apply two coats of that. It works almost as well.

For painting the head, proceed as follows.

2. Prepare a batch of your "base" color, mixing enough to cover all the heads, with some left over for patching and touch-up jobs. Put some aside in an airtight container; you'll use this to paint over the various injuries that your puppets will sustain in the course of their stage careers. You'll be able to prepare a satisfactory Caucasian flesh color with a mixture of yellow, red, umber, and white.

Fig. 2-21. Well-molded papier-mâché heads catch the light and cast interesting shadows.

36

Fig. 2-22. *A puppet is not a doll.*

3. Place a quantity of the base color in a separate container and adjust it to suit the character you're working on. Paint the entire surface of the head with it.

4. Mix a darker version of your base color by adding a small amount of umber or black. Brush this into any wrinkles or sunken areas that you want to emphasize, blending them at the edges into the basic fleshtone, exactly as if you were applying makeup.

5. Mix a lighter tone and use this to highlight raised surfaces.

6. Finally, paint in the whites and pupils of the eyes, and any other details. If you want, you can put a lifelike glint in the puppet's eyes by gluing a black sequin in the middle of each pupil. This will catch the light and make the marionette look alive.

The head is now finished—except for one thing. Your puppet is still bald, unless you've carved or modeled a hairstyle directly onto his head. In Chapter V we'll discuss different types of wigs and hats you can make for your marionette. But for now, put heads out of your head, and start thinking about how your marionette should look, and move, from the neck down (FIG. 2-22).

III

The Body

I became...capable of bestowing animation upon senseless matter.

Frankenstein
Mary Wollstonecraft Shelley

SCIENCE FICTION WRITERS HAVE ALWAYS BEEN PREOCCUPIED WITH ROBOTS and androids, and lately we've been seeing a lot of that kind of thing in the movies. But our civilization is certainly not the first to show an interest in artificial life. The impulse to recreate the human form is probably as old as history. There's something inherently fascinating about a manmade thing that looks real. And when the copy not only looks human but also moves and speaks in a lifelike way, fascination turns to wonder and delight.

It is hardly surprising that archaeologists have found jointed wooden and clay figurines in ancient Greek temples and Egyptian tombs, or that some churches in medieval England were equipped with articulated statues—religious sculptures with moving parts. It's difficult to say what purpose these served, but for many they must have fulfilled the common human wish to see inanimate matter behave as if it had the spark of life. That wish has ensured the continuing popularity of clockwork automatons, animated cartoons, and electronic robots. It has also kept the wooden marionette in business for over 400 years.

The illusion of lifelike movement is the puppeteer's stock in trade. And it is in this that the wooden string puppet surpasses all others. Some kinds of puppets move more swiftly and some move more precisely, but none so faithfully reproduces the full range of human gestures. The key to the marionette's extraordinary versatility is its jointed body. The more fully articulated the puppet's body, the more powerful the illusion that he is alive. And anyone who has seen a well-planned marionette show knows just how compelling that illusion can be (FIG. 3-1).

Many people attribute the power of that illusion to the puppeteer's skill, and not without reason. A skilled puppeteer can animate practically anything—a banana, a bootjack, a bottle brush. Few people realize, however, that the way a puppet *moves* has a lot to do with the way it is *made*. It is the puppet maker who decides what actions a puppet will be able to perform. It is the maker who determines whether the puppet will use abrupt, furtive gestures or wide, sweeping ones. It is the maker who decides whether the puppet will have a stooped posture and shuffling gait, or an upright and noble bearing.

Appropriate movements should be built into the puppet. The best marionettes always seem to look right, no matter what the puppeteer does with them. In fact, a good marionette should look natural even when flung down at random. This means that it should not do anything anatomically improbable—its arms and legs should be unable to bend the wrong way, and its head should not turn backward. It should spring to life the very instant the manipulator takes the control.

This, by the way, is what differentiates *real* marionettes—i.e., homemade marionettes—from the cheap string puppets that are sold in some toy shops. There are a lot of unusable marionettes on the market (most seem to originate in Mexico, for some reason). Because they are so badly built, they've given string puppets an undeserved reputation for being difficult to manipulate. Typically, they have no internal structure, so they tangle easily and are practically impossible to control. Children quickly become frustrated and consign them to the bottom of the toybox, where they lie, hopelessly snarled, waiting for a yard sale. By contrast, a properly made string puppet will hold a child's attention for hours, and even small children can avoid tangles. Oddly, I've never seen commercially made marionettes that meet this standard.

A puppet's body should not only move well, it should express his character. String puppeteers are sometimes asked if they ever recycle marionette bodies by removing one head and attaching another. In fact, it is almost never practical to do this, because every puppet is designed differently. Each one is built to look and move in a way that is consistent with the particular role he is playing. This doesn't mean you have to reinvent the marionette for every puppet you make. If you want to build a puppet whose hips wiggle a certain way, you might find you have to design a special hip-wiggling mechanism yourself. In most cases, though, making your puppet body unique will entail minor adaptations to the basic puppet design.

In this chapter, I'll provide plans and instructions for making a generic marionette. Most of the characters you might wish to attempt will be variations on the standard body type and stringing arrangement. This design is extremely versatile, so your first puppet should be of this type. In later chapters we'll look at designs for specialized marionettes that are capable of juggling or playing the fiddle.

40

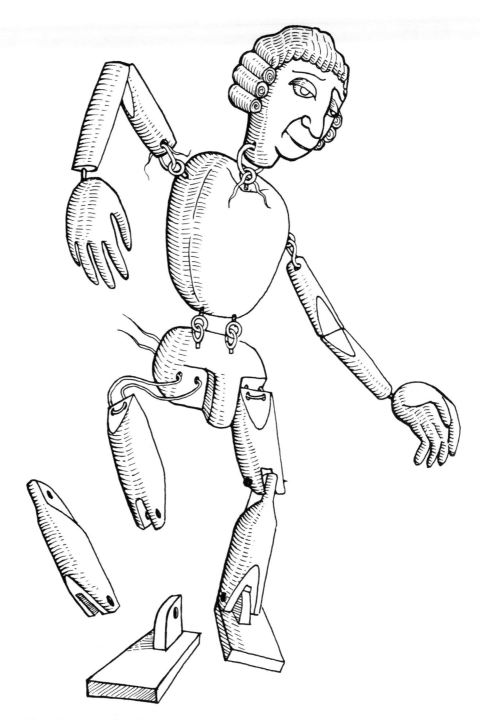

Fig. 3-1. A typical marionette body.

THE PERFECT BODY

If you began by modeling your marionette's head, you should have a good idea of what his body will look like. You might even have sketched a full-length portrait in full costume. So much the better. This chapter should enable you to design a working physique for the puppet you have imagined. When you're ready to start carving the body, you'll find it useful to work from a full-sized diagram. For now, though, concentrate on sketching out the basic body shape, while thinking a bit about how the parts will fit together. After you've read this chapter, you'll have a pretty good idea how a typical wooden string puppet is made. To some extent, simple mechanics will dictate to you what is and isn't possible, which movements the puppet can perform and which movements are impractical. For the time being, just assume that anything is possible and imagine the character as if it were alive.

To start with, ask yourself what actions this character will need to perform. If you are making a fairy, it might need a set of wings. Of course you can just glue them onto your finished puppet later, but they'll look a lot more balanced if you plan the whole puppet, right from the start, with those wings in mind. Maybe your character spends all his time sitting down and never needs to stand up. In that case, you can probably save yourself the trouble of carving legs for him.

As we've already mentioned, every puppet will have its own particular way of moving and its own bodily proportions. In most cases these will reflect the puppet's character. A bully might have short legs, wide shoulders, and long arms. He might have enormous hands that swing from side to side as he swaggers up and down (FIG. 3-2).

A very old man might be frail and spindly. He will probably have stooped shoulders. He might walk with small, careful steps, as if he is afraid of falling over (FIG. 3-3). You might be able to think of other features that would convey an impression of advanced age. For instance, you might give him legs that are always slightly bent. Or you might design the puppet so that he tends to hold his hands quite close together. It's hard to say why these traits connote frailty, but they are very effective.

Good puppeteers, like mimes and cartoonists, develop a sensitivity to physical traits. Often a puppet's body language can say more about his character than his face or clothing. The two puppets in the following drawing have identical bodies, but they carry themselves differently. Because of this, one seems timid and mousy, the other brash and outgoing (FIG. 3-4).

The key to conveying character through physical type is *exaggeration*. Subtle body effects won't read from a distance. Delicately modeled belly folds, individually carved ribs, and other fine touches will tend to disappear in the puppet's clothing. Don't hold back. If you're going to put a hump on his back, make it a big one.

The same general rule applies in anything to do with puppets: if you want to say something, say it loud and clear. Don't add minute details to the body or costume of the puppet just for the sake of having more detail. Dainty handiwork looks lovely on those porcelain dolls that sit under glass bells, but on a

Fig. 3-2. A bully.

Fig. 3-3. A frail old man.

Fig. 3-4. Body language can make a big difference.

marionette every feature should command the attention and contribute some information about where the creature comes from, what he represents, and who he is. If the character does a lot of sneezing, by all means give him a handkerchief (just make sure it can be seen from the back row); but there's probably no need to give him a pocket watch as well. In all things, be governed by what the character needs to do in his or her story.

Of course, if you have no intention of putting on a show then you might wish to ignore this advice. But even so, you will probably find that an excess of detail gives the puppet a decorated look, which detracts from his "personhood."

Once you know exactly how the puppet will look and move, you should make a life-sized pencil sketch of his body, showing how all the wooden components will fit together. However, there's no point in attempting this until you've read the rest of the chapter, so lay aside your pencil and prepare for a lesson in puppet anatomy.

HIPS AND TORSO

An octopus can bend every which way; therefore an octopus puppet can be a relatively unstructured affair. A puppet-human is another matter. As the possessor of a human body, you must have noticed certain limitations. Your arms bend one way, but not the other; your head, thank goodness, is incapable of swivelling 180 degrees around. You probably cannot touch your nose with your elbow, or the back of your head with the sole of your foot. To look natural, a marionette should reproduce all of those existing limitations, without introducing any new ones. FIGURE 3-5 shows a marionette that will do this well.

An enlarged version of this drawing could serve as your full-scale working diagram. If you have not already done so, make a simple sketch showing the front and side view of the puppet. This doesn't have to be beautifully drawn, or even particularly detailed, as long as it shows the correct proportions for the main components of the puppet body. You are now ready to begin work on the hips and torso.

Tools and Materials

- Block of softwood, approximately 6 × 2 ½ × 3 ½ inches.
- Soft pencil.
- Vise. (A good vise is essential for dealing with small pieces of wood.)
- Handsaw. (A narrow-bladed handsaw, suitable for fine work is indispensable. For marionette making, a Japanese "Dozuki," a type of backsaw is excellent. A number of western-style saws are also suitable, such as dovetail or slotting saws, keyhole saws and coping saws. Hobby shops often carry small sawblades for miniatures and model building, which are excellent for cutting the slots in marionette leg joints.)
- Screw eyes.
- Wood rasp and/or coarse sandpaper.
- Nylon string.
- Needle-nosed pliers.

---

1. Use a fine-grained softwood for the hips and torso of your puppet. You will not be doing any fine carving on the upper body, so almost any wood will do, provided it is reasonably light and easy to work. Select a block with no large knots and cut it into two smaller blocks, corresponding to the trunk and the pelvis (FIG. 3-6).

The measurements in FIG. 3-6 are appropriate for a puppet of slight build, standing about 17 inches high. You should feel free to alter the proportions if

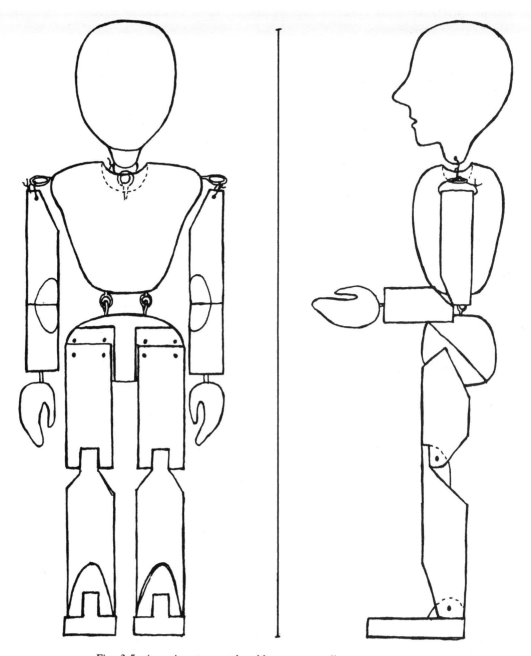

Fig. 3-5. A marionette must be able to move well.

it suits your purposes, but bear in mind that the exact outlines of the puppet's body need not be carved into the wood. If you are making a chubby puppet, for example, you might begin by making an ordinary, well-proportioned body and then fatten him up later by gluing small pads of polyurethane directly to his wooden

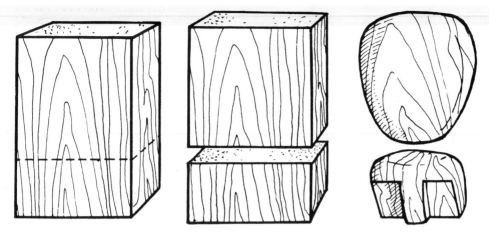

Fig. 3-6. Guidelines for making the pelvis.

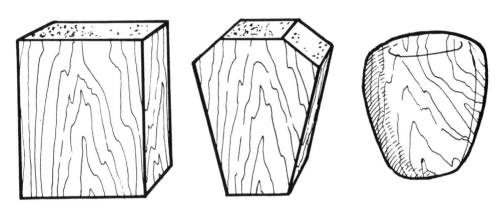

Fig. 3-7. Guidelines for making the torso.

torso. In most cases, your work will be covered up by the puppet's clothing, so it doesn't matter if he looks a bit scrappy and patched together.

2.   Shape the upper torso out of the larger of your two blocks, using a saw, rasps, and heavy sandpaper. The exact form is not especially important, as long as the shoulders are wider than the waist. The arms will hang freely from the shoulders, and they should move without obstruction from the chest or stomach (FIG. 3-7).

3.   The hips are a bit trickier. Draw guidelines in pencil directly on the surface of the block (FIG. 3-8).

4.   Make the angled cuts first, sawing in from the side toward the center. Stop at the vertical line.

5.   Cut down at an angle from the vertical line which marks the edge of the crotch. Remove the wedge of waste wood (FIG. 3-9).

6.   Repeat on the other side. You now have the rough shape of the pelvis, with two angled slots where the puppet's thighs will be attached (FIG. 3-10).

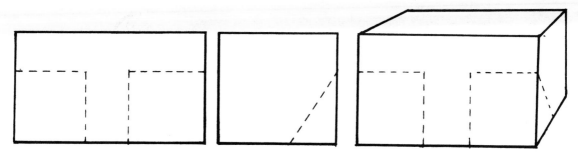

Fig. 3-8. Guidelines for making the hips.

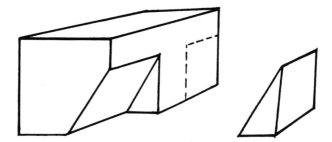

Fig. 3-9. Make angled cuts carefully.

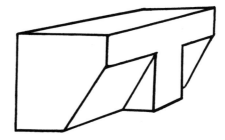

Fig. 3-10. Slots for attaching the legs.

7.   Now round out the hips using saw, rasp and sandpaper. The block should be approximately oval in shape, as seen from above or below (FIG. 3-11).

8.   Attach the pelvis to the trunk with four interlocking screw eyes, as in the following diagram (FIG. 3-12). The screw eyes can be easily opened up with a pair of needle-nosed pliers, and then closed again to form the links. Note: For the sake of your puppet's posture, position the screw eyes so that the hips hang straight, without sagging at the front or the back.

LEGS

After you finish the pelvis, it's time for some leg work. Proceed as follows. To make arms and legs, you'll need most of the materials listed for the torso and pelvis, as well as those listed on the following page.

Fig. 3-11. Round out the hips.

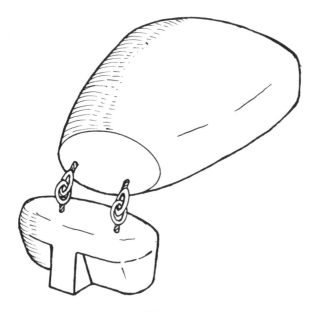

Fig. 3-12. Attach the pelvis to the trunk with screw eyes.

50

1.   The thigh and the calf of the leg will be notched together in a simple tongue-and-groove joint, hinged with a ¾-inch finishing nail. The upper thigh will be laced to the pelvis with a piece of string.

2.   Start with a piece of ¾- or 1-inch dowelling, roughly 3 ½ inches in length (again, the proportions are up to you). Cut an angle into the upper thigh as follows (FIG. 3-13). Make the cut quite steep, if the angle is too wide, the legs will not hang vertically from the pelvis.

3.   Make a shorter angled cut on the front of the leg (FIG. 3-14).

4.   The upper part of the thigh is finished. Place the thigh in a clamp with the knee end pointing up. Cut a slot about ½ inch deep, perpendicular to the sloping cut you have made in the upper thigh. The width of this slot should be about one third of the diameter of the dowelling (FIG. 3-15). Remove the wood-

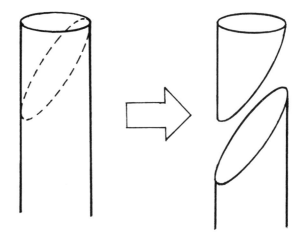

Fig. 3-13. Cut dowelling for the upper thigh.

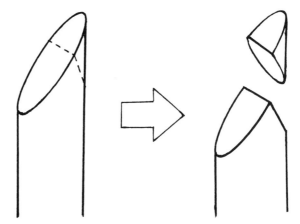

Fig. 3-14. Cut dowelling for the front of the leg.

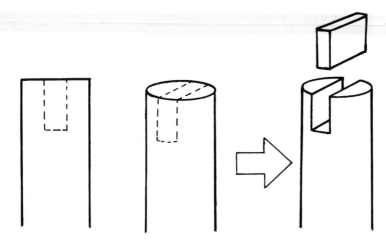

Fig. 3-15. Cut a slot in the dowel.

en plug at the center of the slot with a chisel. If you don't have a small enough chisel, another way is to make repeated vertical sawcuts inside the slot, until the plug is reduced to slivers that can be easily broken off and removed.

  5. Make a sloping cut (similar to the one on the upper thigh) from a little behind the knee to the back of the leg (FIG. 3-16). Make sure to start the cut about ¼ inch behind the knee, so that, as seen from the side, the knee does not end in a sharp point (FIG. 3-17).

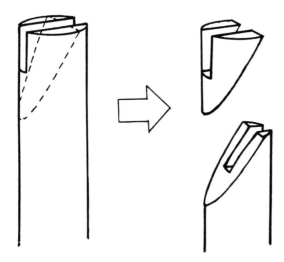

Fig. 3-16. Make a sloping cut on the leg dowel.

  6. Put the upper leg aside and take another piece of dowelling, from which you will make the calf and ankle. On one end of this you are going to cut the "tongue," which fits into the slot on the thigh. Place the lower leg in your clamp and make two vertical cuts, each about ½ inch long, as in the diagram. Then make two horizontal cuts and remove the extra wood (FIG. 3-18).

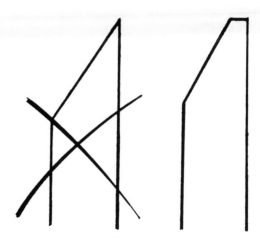

Fig. 3-17. The knee should not end in a sharp point.

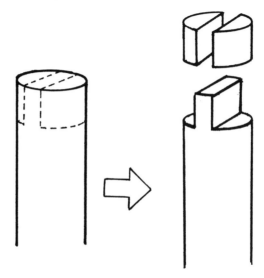

Fig. 3-18. This tongue on the calf dowel will fit into the slot on the thigh.

7. You now have a rectangular tongue that projects above the cylindrical dowel. Make another sloping cut to remove the back of the calf. As on the thigh, start the cut ¼ inch or so behind the knee, so that the top surface of the tongue is not pointed, but square (FIG. 3-19). Round out the back of the tongue, leaving the front as is.

8. The basic shape of the knee is finished, but you will almost certainly have some fine tuning to do. Test the joint by inserting the tongue on the calf into the groove on the thigh. If the tongue is too wide to enter easily, carefully shave it down (or else enlarge the slot). When the tongue moves in the slot without too much friction, it is time to drill a hole for the hinge nail.

Fig. 3-19. Make a sloping cut for the back of the calf.

9. Fit the tongue into the groove, setting it in as deeply as it will go. Now wrap the joint with a few turns of masking tape, so that the two parts of the leg do not move around as you are drilling them out (FIG. 3-20).

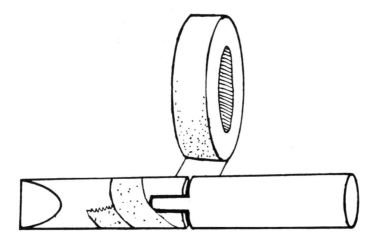

Fig. 3-20. Wrap joint with masking tape to prevent movement as you drill.

10. Drill a hole right through the knee, taking care that it passes through both wings of the thigh slot as well as the tongue of the knee slot. (Proceed cautiously, holding the drill straight up and down. If the hole is drilled at the wrong angle the joint might be stiff or fragile). Remove the masking tape and insert the finishing nail hinge. The knee is more or less complete.

11. You'll probably find that the knee is a bit stiff and it is likely that it will not bend properly. If this is the case, your puppet needs corrective surgery. Examine the joint carefully to see what is impeding the movement of the leg. Use sandpaper and a carving knife to remove the obstructions. It might be that the two sloping cuts on the back of the leg are not steep enough to allow the leg to bend properly. If the problem is caused by fat thighs, trim them down and the legs should work fine. When the knee is finished it should bend backward

quite easily, but it should be *unable to bend forward*. Make sure that all is well and then proceed to the ankles.

12.   The ankle joint is a lot like the knee joint, except that it must bend the opposite way. That is, the sloping part of the joint will be on the front of the lower leg instead of the back. Examine how your own foot bends. Make a slot on the lower end of the calf, exactly like the one you made on the lower end of the thigh (FIG. 3-21).

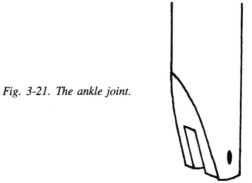

Fig. 3-21. The ankle joint.

13.   It is possible to carve feet out of a single block of hardwood or dowelling. An easier way is to begin by carving a small hardwood tongue to fit into the ankle slot on the lower leg (FIG. 3-22). The shape of the ankle tongue is quite important. It should not be perfectly rounded at the top, or else the foot will droop when the puppet lifts his leg (FIG. 3-23).

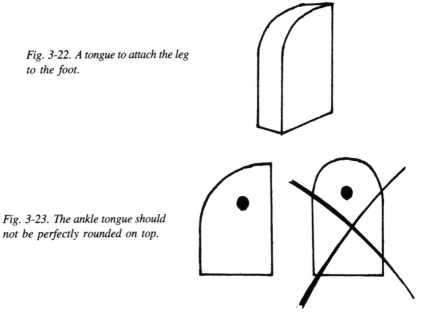

Fig. 3-22. A tongue to attach the leg to the foot.

Fig. 3-23. The ankle tongue should not be perfectly rounded on top.

14. Cut a slot in a flat piece of wood about 2 ½ inches in length and ¼ inch high. Glue the bottom flat edge of the tongue into this slot. Drill and hinge the foot to the ankle, exactly as you did the knee (FIG. 3-24).

15. By now your puppet has a functional, if rather inelegant, foot. Later on you can use papier-mache or polyurethane foam to make him a pair of boots or overshoes.

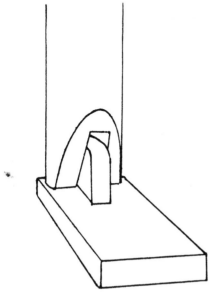

Fig. 3-24. The tongue in place.

16. The legs are fastened to the pelvis by strong nylon string. Attaching them is a simple business. First, drill two holes very near to the top the thigh. The size of the holes depends on how thick your string is. Then drill two holes right through the pelvis from the front to the back. Space these so that they re as far apart as the two holes on the thigh. Finally, lace the thighs to the pelvis, using a synthetic fibre string (black woven fishing line, 30 pounds test, works very well). Leave enough slack to allow the thigh to bend up, but not so much that the legs wobble around (FIG. 3-25).

ARMS

Arms, you'll be happy to hear, are a lot simpler than legs. Use smaller dowelling (½ to ⅝ inch). The length of the arm segments is up to you, but as a general rule the puppet's arm, including the hand, will extend from the shoulder to the top of the knee joint.

1. You can make the elbow joint in the same way as the knee joint, but there is an easier method which works equally well. Cut a slice out of the upper and lower arms, exactly as on the backs of the legs (FIG. 3-26). Then simply glue a cloth or leather "hinge" to the inside of the arm. Use a small strip of any strong flexible material. Afterwards, paint it the same color as the arm (FIG. 3-27).

56

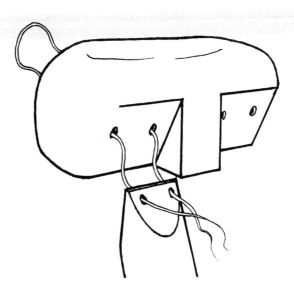

Fig. 3-25. Fasten leg to pelvis with strong nylon string.

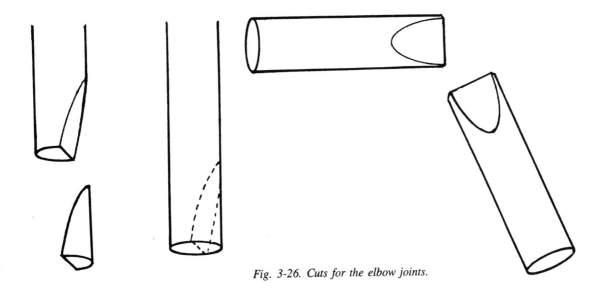

Fig. 3-26. Cuts for the elbow joints.

I've found that it is possible to make a strong (and rather unsightly) elbow hinge entirely out of cloth-backed adhesive tape. Because cloth joints are less attractive than the tongue and-groove type, you should use them only on marionettes whose arms will be covered up by long sleeves.

2. The human shoulder joint is an ingenious contrivance, permitting the arms to swivel freely in all directions. On a marionette you can mimic this action

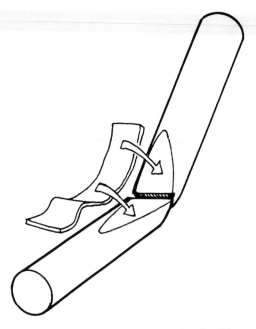

Fig. 3-27. Use cloth hinges instead of wooden ones only when hinge will be covered by the marionette's clothing.

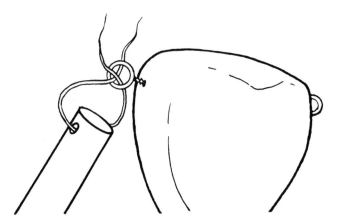

Fig. 3-28. Attaching the marionette's arm.

by lacing the upper arm to a screw eye mounted on the shoulder. Begin by drilling a hole near the top of the arm. Then tie the arms to a screw eye mounted on the puppet's shoulder with nylon string or fishing line (FIG. 3-28).

3. There is usually no need for a moveable wrist joint. Hands can be mounted directly on the ends of the forearms. If for some reason your puppet must have freely moving hands however, these can be fastened to the wrists by interlocking screw eyes. If you are making hands out of wire and masking tape, the wires can be twisted around a small screw eye on the wrists.

HANDS

After the face, the hands are the most expressive parts of the human body. On a puppet, they can actually be more expressive than the face, because they move. A marionette's face is frozen into one fixed attitude; to compensate for that, the hands must be all the more expressive. Because so much of a puppet's expression must come from its hands, they should be made large enough to catch and hold the audience's attention. A common beginner's mistake is to make the hands and feet too small. This error is most disturbing when the puppet has a large head. There's something plainly monstrous about a big-headed puppet with small hands and feet; it is as if the head and body of two different creatures have somehow gotten mixed up. The larger the head in relation to the body the larger the extremities should be.

If you have plenty of time, you might wish to carve the hands out of wood. Otherwise you can make a fine pair of hands in under an hour, using wire and masking tape.

Masking tape actually has several advantages over wood. In the first place, this method makes it easy to shape very durable hands with delicate, separated fingers. In the second place, the finished masking tape hands remain flexible, which allows you to change their shape at any time before—or even during—the performance. This is useful if the puppet has to do something special with this hands during a given scene in a play, such as make a fist, or scoop up a basket. As the following instructions show, masking tape hands are not difficult to make.

1.   Take a length of wire and bend it into the shape of a hand. You may find it helpful to work from a full-sized drawing, so that you know how long to make each finger and so on. After you've made the basic shape of a hand with fingers and thumb, pass the wire across the palm and back of the hand a few times to reinforce the structure. Twist the ends together at the wrist (FIG. 3-29).

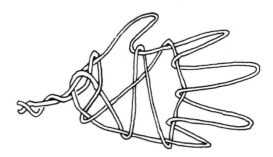

Fig. 3-29. Form the hand out of wire.

2.   Make the second wire hand shape right away, before going on to the next stage. Use the first hand as a guide, so that the two hands are identical.

3.   Wrap a few strips of masking tape around the palm of the hand. To give the palm and the base of the thumb more volume you can insert wads of cotton or folded newspaper, secured with strips of masking tape.

4. As the shape develops, tear off smaller pieces of masking tape. Apply these to the hand and fingers one at a time, building the shape gradually. Do your best to create a smooth surface with no bulges or flaps of tape sticking out

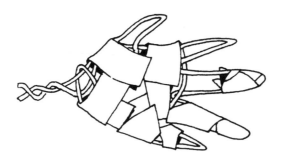

Fig. 3-30. Cover the wire hand form with masking tape.

Fig. 3-31. A puppet's hand, made out of wire and masking tape. The string on the fingertips prevents the puppet's hands from snagging other strings. (Photograph by Jano Salinas.)

(FIG. 3-30). If you accidentally create a lump, there's no need to undo any of your work. Just cut off the mistake with a pair of scissors and patch the gap with more masking tape.

5. Apply several thick coats of gesso to smooth out the surface. Paint the hand at the same time as you do the face and any other unclothed parts of the body (FIG. 3-31).

6. Attach the hands to the forearms with glue and masking tape. If your puppet must have articulated wrists, twist the wrist wires around small screw eyes mounted on the ends of the forearm.

ATTACHING THE HEAD

The head is laced to a medium-sized screw eye on the puppet's shoulders. It is a good idea to gouge out a small hole in between the shoulders for the screw eye to sit in. This hides the screw eye and also keeps the neck from looking outlandishly long. Tie both ends of the lace to the screw eye. If you simply pass the string through the screw eye and tie it to itself, the head will not sit perfectly straight on the body (FIG. 3-32).

Some puppeteers prefer to join the neck to the shoulders with two interlocking screw eyes. The advantage of this is that it keeps the head from swinging wildly in all directions; the disadvantage is that it prevents the head from swinging *controllably* in all directions. You would do better to lace the neck to the shoulders, and then, if the head swings from side to side too easily, you can "stiffen" the neck by adding some cloth stuffing under the puppet's collar.

Another way to join the head to the body is to dispense with screw eyes entirely and give the puppet a rope neck. I'll describe how to do this in Chapter IV.

COSMETIC SURGERY

Dr. Frankenstein named his creature "Beautiful," and was deeply disappointed that it was not. At this stage you might be having similar misgivings about the being you have created. The body is in working order, the limbs are functionally complete—and yet the poor thing looks unnatural.

The main problem is that the arms and legs are still, basically, just tubes of wood, no thinner at the ankles and wrists than they are at the thighs and biceps. So the whole puppet gives the impression of having been strung together like so many sausages. This won't matter much if the puppet is to be dressed in loose clothing. But if he is to have bare limbs, you should do what you can to make them look realistic.

Whittle down the wrists and lower leg so that they are thinner than the upper arm and thighs. A penknife will suffice for this work, but it is most easily done with an electric rasp or a rotary power tool. Round the back of the calf and carve out the area around the knee, being careful not to chop anything essential from the joints. Remove sharp edges and artificial-looking contours. In short, make him look human (FIG. 3-33).

You can drastically alter the shape of the body by gluing strips of foam rubber to it. Of course, this can only be done on parts of the body that will be covered

Fig. 3-32. Attaching the head.

by clothing. Use contact cement, airplane glue, or any other adhesive that works on synthetic materials. An excellent tool for working with foam rubber is an electric glue gun. (In Chapter V, I'll describe how glue guns work and what they are good for.) Build the foam up in thick layers and then "sculpt" it with a pair of ordinary scissors (see the section on foam hats in Chapter V). Take care not to place any foam rubber where it will obstruct the free movement of the shoulder or pelvis joints.

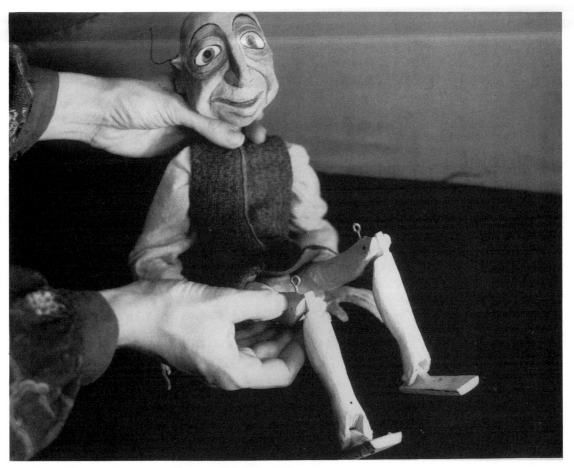

Fig. 3-33. Dressing the puppet. (Photograph by Jano Salinas.)

Padding the bodies with foam has several advantages. To begin with, the finished puppet will be considerably lighter than if he were made entirely of wood. During performances and rehearsals, puppeteers can spend long periods of time holding their marionettes at arm's length over the stage. This is extremely tiring, and can result in shoulder pain and a sore upper back. Foam padding is a good way to make the puppet fat without making him heavy. Also, foam is a lot easier to shape than wood, so it gives you more control over the puppet's silhouette. Finally, it is easier to make tight-fitting clothes for a foam-bodied puppet, because the foam rubber can be compressed while the clothing is being applied, giving your puppet the soft, rounded look of a real mammal.

There is one last thing to do before moving on to the next stage: paint all parts of the body that will not be covered up by clothing. As I mentioned in the previous chapter, this should be done at the same time as you paint the head, using the same batch of mixed paint. If this is inconvenient, mix a good quantity of flesh tone and set some aside in an airtight container. Most types of paint can be stored for a short time under these conditions. Brush a layer of gesso on the hands, wrists, ankles and shoulders—any part of the puppet that will be exposed to the audience. Apply a uniform layer of mixed paint and leave to dry. If necessary, add more layers until the surface is completely covered and none of the white from the gesso shines through.

IV

Stringing Up

Then ductile wires are added to command
Its motions governed by a nimble hand.
And now, directed by a hand unseen,
The finished puppet struts before the scene.

"A Puppet Show" (1716)
Joseph Addison

IN SOME FORMS OF PUPPETRY THE MANIPULATOR SHARES THE STAGE WITH THE puppet, making little attempt to conceal himself. But string marionettes usually have the spotlight to themselves, while the puppeteer keeps out of sight behind a curtain or backdrop. The marionette's strings are the only link between the puppeteer and the miniature world that is spread out below him. With these he exerts total control over that world without intruding upon it (FIG. 4-1).

A good marionette leaves very little to chance. Its strings are arranged so that the user enjoys complete mastery over all its movements. Arriving at a satisfactory way of stringing up is largely a matter of experiment and personal preference. A marionette can have as few as five strings or as many as fifty. It depends on what you want. A five-stringed puppet will be easy to manipulate, but the range of its movements will be severely limited. A fifty-stringed puppet will be able to perform all kinds of subtle maneuvers, but taking advantage of them might be difficult.

It will take you longer to learn to manipulate a many-stringed marionette, and even then you might not have much use for all the finicky gestures your puppet can perform. You might even find that those extra strings detract from the quality of your show. What you gain in realism you could lose in speed and responsiveness. Even a sympathetic spectator will start to fidget in his seat, waiting for your marionette to roll his eyes in their sockets or waggle his independently articulated fingers. So make it a rule to keep your puppets as simple as you can

Fig. 4-1. Cathy Stubington of the Picardi Marionette Theatre manipulating a puppet. (Photograph by Jano Salinas.)

make them, without sacrificing important movements. "Important" movements are simply those which advance the action of the play. Don't give your puppet blinking eyes or a mouth that moves when he talks unless there is a good reason for calling attention to these features. Getting a laugh is a pretty good reason; impressing the audience with the puppet's dexterity is not.

Most beginners err on the side of fussiness, aiming for a precise duplication of human movements. That's not necessarily a bad thing; realistic gestures are delightful when they happen swiftly and without obvious effort. However, all too often the audience is made to sit through an unending series of difficult and precarious maneuvers. From the puppeteer's point of view, this might constitute a real virtuoso performance. From where the audience sits, it will be slightly more frustrating than watching somebody put a frayed thread through the eye of a needle. Puppetry, after all, is theatre, and "timing" is every bit as important to a wooden performer as to a human one. Lose your timing and you'll lose your audience.

Having muttered all these dark warnings on the perils of under-simplification, I should point out that complex gestures don't have to use up a lot of time. They can be built into the puppet's strings so that they happen almost automatically. A fine-tuned marionette has built-in poise and equilibrium, and will leap to life the moment you take its control. Merely tilting the wooden control will cause the puppet to bend over, bow its head, and kneel. Tilt it another way and the marionette will turn its face upwards, cock it's head to one side and seem to clasp its hands in prayer. This is possible because of the way the strings are positioned on the wooden crosspieces of the control. The builder can do a lot of the puppeteer's work for him by setting things up so that individual strings function in unison. If the puppet is strung up correctly, you won't need nine arms to manipulate him gracefully.

There are few rules that apply to the building of a marionette control. The main purpose of the control is to keep all the strings separate, so that the puppeteer can find the one he wants with his free hand. There are several different ways to do this, and with a bit of trial and error you'll soon find the one that works best for you. In the following pages I'll describe a simple stringing system that is well suited to the basic puppet body you built in the last chapter.

There are two main types of marionette control (FIG. 4-2). The first, called a "crutch control" (A), is held vertically and assembled from sticks of dowelling. The other, called the "airplane" type (B), is held horizontally and made of flat pieces of lattice wood. Both styles have been in use for several centuries, and for the average puppeteer, there is little to choose between them.

Many skilled manipulators find the crutch control more versatile than the airplane, because of the way it is held. The crutch is supported in the crook between the thumb and the index finger, leaving a few of the fingers free to do some manipulating. For instance, the hand that holds the crutch can operate the two metal rods of the "walking" mechanism.

The airplane control is held from above, like the handle of a suitcase, so the hand that supports the control can do little else. Despite this limitation, the horizontal control is generally easier to make and use, especially for beginning

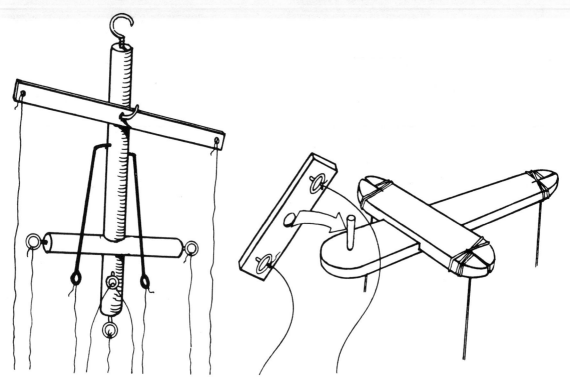

Fig. 4-2. Two types of marionette control.

puppeteers. The strings on the airplane are fairly widely spaced, so there is little danger that the manipulator will grab the wrong one by mistake. Furthermore, there are ways to build the control so that the puppeteer can make some use of the supporting hand.

For these reasons I'll confine my detailed explanations to the airplane control. By the time you are ready to experiment with the crutch control, you will be well past the stage where you need such explanations anyway. (We'll return to the vertical or "crutch" control in Chapter VI, because there are some feats which a horizontal control just can't duplicate).

Before setting to work on the control, you must decide what parts of the puppet's anatomy need to move. In a very plain marionette these will be the head, the hands, the back, and the legs. These four parts of the body will almost always require strings, although some puppets can get by with no strings on their legs, as we'll see presently. Special marionettes will require special strings—a dog will have a tail-wagging thread, and an angel will have strings on its wings.

After you've determined what needs to move, you must figure out how it should move. Is it enough that the hands can go up and down, or will you need to draw them in toward the body? Do the wrists have to bend? Finally, are there any basic strings you can do without?

If the puppet is to wear a gown or a long dress, there will be no need to attach leg strings. The legs will be hidden, so there's no point in "walking" the puppet. Reasoning along these lines, you might conclude that this kind of puppet can do without legs completely. However, there are two excellent reasons for including legs, even if the audience never sees them. First, legs give a natural-looking shape to the puppet's costume; without them, the empty gown is apt to crumple grotesquely under the weight of the marionette's body. Second, legs help prevent puppet levitation—a frequent and somewhat unnerving distraction in some puppet shows. Solid wooden legs allow the puppeteer to feel that the soles of the feet are flat on the stage floor.

A SIMPLE STRINGING SYSTEM

"Stringing up" is one of the decisive moments in the art of the marionette. It is to the puppeteer what "hoisting the mainsail" is to a pirate. To prevent this momentous occasion from lapsing into slapstick comedy, I recommend that you ask somebody to help you with the final part of the task, that of connecting the puppet to the wooden control.

One person should stand on a chair and hold the control while the other attaches the strings. The puppet strings are longer than any one person's arms, and there will be many adjustments to make at both ends of the control. It can be a frustrating job if you go about it the wrong way. If nobody is available to help you, don't attempt to attach the strings with the puppet lying flat on the ground. That will not end well. Drive a nail or cup hook into the top of a doorframe and hang the control in the open doorway. This, by the way, is the key to preventing tangles in everything you do with the puppets. It can be stated as a simple, but important, rule: *leave them hanging*. As long as the marionettes are dangling freely from their airplanes, it is impossible for them to get snarled up, but if you lay them out flat, drop the control, or wind the strings around the body, they will become tangled without fail.

The length of the strings is up to you. It depends on two things: your height and the way your stage is set up. Generally, you should make the strings short enough that you will not have to hold your hands much above waist level, and long enough that you will not have to stoop. If you want to be really scientific about this, use the following rule of thumb: Measure the distance between the "bridge" (where the performers stand) and the stage floor (where the puppets stand), and add that to the distance from your waist to the ground. Add 7 inches and subtract the height of the puppet. That will give you the length of the head string. It might also give you a headache. If so, abandon science and resort to good old trial and error.

1.   The marionette control can be as simple as a piece of lattice wood, 7 to 9 inches long, with a single crosspiece (FIG. 4-3).

2.   If you wish, you could go to the trouble of notching the two slats of wood together (FIG. 4-4). An electric router would be useful for this. Otherwise, the slats can be glued together with ordinary white glue and made fast with carpet tacks, wood staples, or small nails. Round off each end of the wooden slat as in FIG. 4-3. This is to prevent the "airplane" from snagging other puppets' strings

during the show. Finally, attach a strip of leather or strong cloth to the top of the centerpiece. This is used to hang the marionette on a rack when it is not in use.

3. Two strings FIG. 4-5A run from the sides of the puppet's head to the two ends of the crosspiece. The crosspiece should be made with narrow slits, about ½ inch long, in each end (FIG. 4-6). To attach the string, wrap it around the wood a few times and then anchor the free end of the string in the slit. This system allows you to adjust the length of the head strings easily.

4. The head strings (FIG. 4-5A) are tied to screw eyes mounted on each side of the puppet's head. Position the screw eyes so that when the head hangs from them it looks *up*. The nearer the screw eyes are to the front of the puppet's face, the more they will tend to do this. However, try to mount the screw eyes behind the puppet's hairline, where they will not be too conspicuous (FIG. 4-7).

5. Mount another screw eye at the back of the puppet's head. Mount a screw eye on the control, and place it on the bottom surface of the centerpiece, an inch or so behind the crosspiece. Run a string (FIG. 4-5C) between the two screw eyes. Now hold the puppet by the control. When the control is held level, the puppet should gaze straight ahead. If he is still looking up, shorten the back-of-the-head string. If he is looking down, lengthen it.

6. When your puppet is on the level, add a string (FIG. 4-5E) running from his lower back to the back end of the control. This string should not bear any of the puppet's weight when the control is held horizontally. But when the front end of the control is tilted down, it should take up some or all of the puppet's weight, causing him to bend at the waist. If he can't bend very far, the back string is either too slack or the screw eye is mounted too high on his back. (In some cases you might prefer to mount it on his pelvis).

7. One continuous string runs from the thumb of one hand to the thumb of the other, passing through a screw eye on the front end of the control (FIG. 4-5B). This string should be short enough that it pulls the hands slightly forward when the puppet is hanging at rest. This prevents the arms from swinging behind the puppet's back.

Tools and Materials

- Saw.
- Screw eyes.
- Carpet tacks and/or wood staples.
- Small strips of Velcro.
- Glue. (Use white glue for wood, and epoxy or contact cement for Velcro.)
- String. (Puppet string should be strong, yet very fine; Ordinary cotton thread is far too weak: Black nylon thread is better, and if nothing else can be obtained it will do. The best kind of string is black woven fishing line, 15 pounds test. *Don't* use transparent nylon thread or fishing line. Onstage, this will catch glints from the overhead lights and throw them back in the audience's eyes. It is also much less supple than woven string.
- Lattice wood (approximately ¾ × ¼ inch).

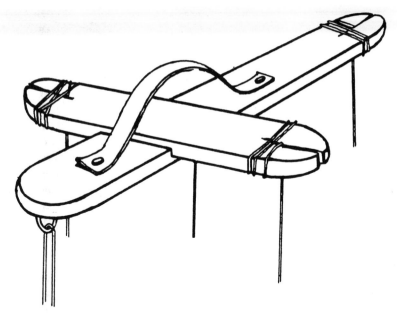

Fig. 4-3. A simple marionette control.

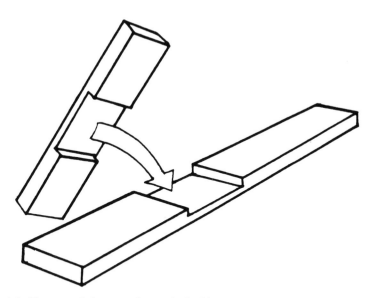

Fig. 4-4. The control slats may be notched with a router.

THE RACK

Most puppeteers are strong proponents of hanging, and recommend the use of the rack as well. It is a matter of common sense. Now that your puppet has his strings, you will have to find somewhere to store him when he is not being used.

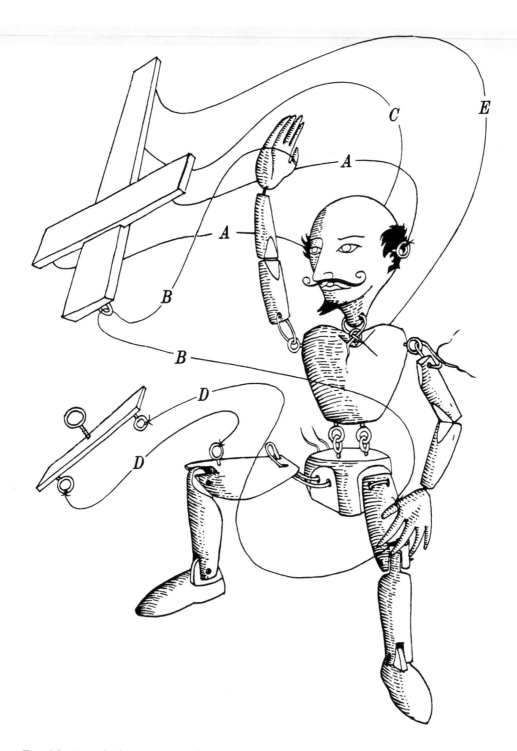

Fig. 4-5. A standard arrangement of strings.

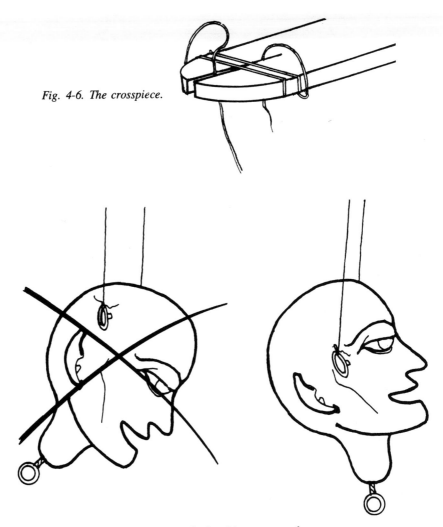

Fig. 4-6. The crosspiece.

Fig. 4-7. Mount the screw eyes so the head hangs properly.

As I've already pointed out, it is not a good idea to leave a string puppet lying down or to permit the control to come anywhere near his body. The most sensible way to store the finished marionettes is to build a rack to dangle them from. What you need is something along the lines of a closet coat rack, with a row of cup hooks on which to hang the controls. If you are planning to tour with your show, you will require a portable puppet rack like the one in FIG. 4-8.

From time to time you will have to pack the puppets away in a hamper or box. It is possible to do this without mishap, but you must take the precaution of tying all the strings together first. Use short pieces of ribbon or shoelace, tying bows at four inch intervals all the way up (FIG. 4-9). Then bundle the puppets in pieces of soft cloth (with the controls *outside* the bundles) and stack the wrapped puppets neatly in the carrying crate.

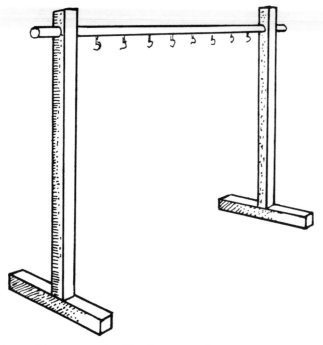

Fig. 4-8. A portable puppet rack will make transporting easy.

WALKING

Most rod or glove puppets have no feet. To make them appear to be walking, the puppeteer bounces them up and down a bit as he glides them along. It is very easy to do, and it doesn't seem to bother the audience that the puppets don't exist from the knees down. Marionettes, however, have legs. The good thing about this is that they can be made to actually walk. The bad news is that they *must* be made to walk—every time they are moved from point A to point B upon the stage. This might not seem to be such a big deal, but in a fast-paced puppet show, it can get to be a bit of a drag (literally). For this reason, it's very important that you develop an easy and convincing way of walking your puppet.

String puppets have a distinctive, some might say peculiar, way of moving; which might explain why nearly every comic mime has a puppet routine in his repertoire. All the same, there is something charming about a puppet's walk, despite the fact that no marionette will ever promenade as gracefully as a real person, any more than it will dance like Fred Astaire. The important thing is to give your marionette a walk that will not distract the audience from other things that are going on.

There are probably as many ways to walk a marionette as there are string puppeteers. Most methods involve attaching a removable crosspiece to the control, as in FIG. 4-10. The crosspiece in the above illustration is fastened to the control with Velcro. White glue will not adhere to Velcro, so you will need to use wood staples, contact cement, or epoxy to attach it to the wood. Alternatively, you can drill a hole in the crosspiece and rest it on a peg of dowelling (FIG. 4-11).

74

Fig. 4-9. When transporting puppets, tie all the strings together to avoid tangles.

Strings run from the removable crosspiece to screw eyes mounted just above the marionette's knees. When it comes time to walk the marionette, the puppeteer lifts the walking stick from its resting place on the control and tilts it first one way and then the other, causing the legs to move up and down as the puppet marches across the stage floor. If all goes well, the puppet's knees will rise to his waist level while his upper body remains straight as a rake, creating an effect that is somewhat reminiscent of the Buckingham Palace guard.

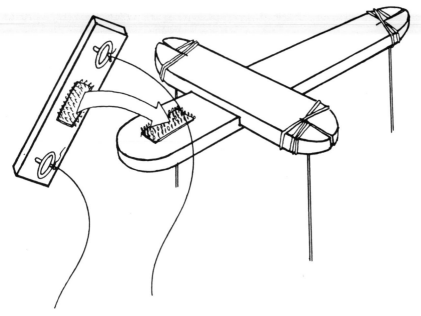

Fig. 4-10. A removable crosspiece using Velcro.

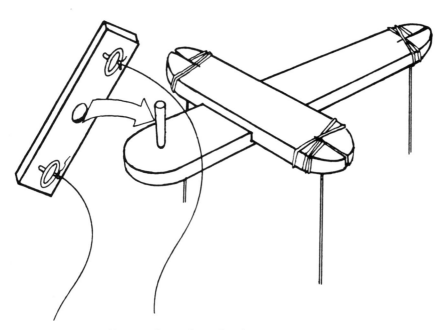

Fig. 4-11. A removable crosspiece using a dowel.

Not everyone likes this effect. Some puppeteers prefer to run the leg string through a screw eye on the knee, tying it to another screw eye mounted on the top of the foot (FIG. 4-12). This straightens the leg and snaps the feet forward, presenting to the audience the unmistakeable illusion that the puppet is performing a military goose step. With practice you will be able to soften the effect a bit, giving the puppet a reasonably civilian appearance, if that is what you want.

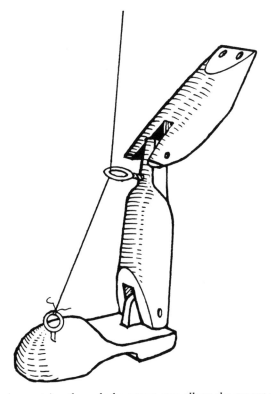

Fig. 4-12. Running a string through the screw eyes allows the puppet to walk.

The main drawback of this approach to walking is that it requires two hands: one to hold the control and the other to hold the walking stick. It is possible to walk the puppet with one hand by mounting the crosspiece on a pivot attached to the centerpiece of the control (FIG. 4-13).

This mechanism is simply a slat of wood bolted to an extension of the central crosspiece. The bolt serves as a pivot for the rocking motion of the crosspiece. (The longer the crosspiece, the more vigorous its action will be.) To use this walking mechanism, you must hold the control in your thumb, ring, and pinkie finger, while rocking the slat with your middle and index fingers (FIG. 4-14). This leaves a hand free to tug at other strings. In return for this convenience, you will probably have to sacrifice a degree of control over your puppet's legs. In most cases this won't matter much. With your free hand you can create subtle

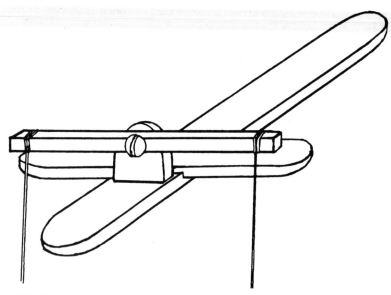

Fig. 4-13. Mounting the crosspiece on a pivot allows you to use one hand instead of two to walk the puppet.

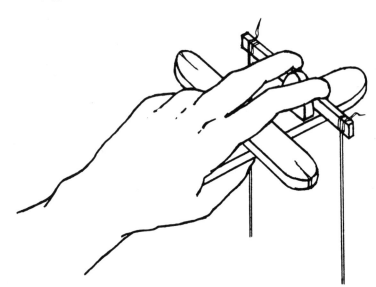

Fig. 4-14. The best way to hold the walking mechanism

movements of the head and hands that will more than compensate for the puppet's poor motor control.

SHOULDER STRINGS

In the simple stringing method given above, the marionette's body literally dangles from its neck. This arrangement afflicts the puppet with a chronic inability to slouch or hunch over—which is fine, if the puppet is playing the part of a vampire or an English nanny. But perfect posture does not look natural on most characters. Fortunately, it can be remedied by the addition of a continuous shoulder string, running from the screw eye on the right shoulder, through a screw eye mounted on the bottom surface of the control, to the screw eye on the left shoulder. The screw eye on the bottom of the control should be placed a little behind the back-of-the-head screw eye (FIG. 4-15).

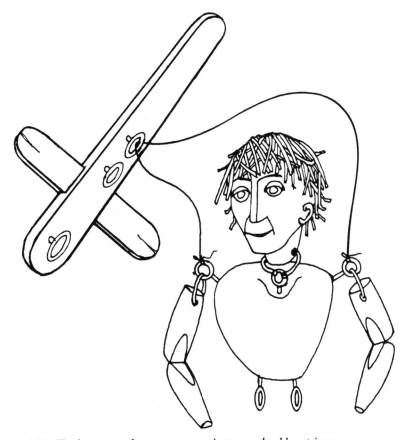

Fig. 4-15. The key to good puppet posture is to use shoulder strings.

If you prefer, the shoulder strings can be made short enough to bear all of the marionette's weight. Otherwise, they can be attached so that they take the puppet's weight only when you tilt the control forward. This will cause the head to drop somewhat more dramatically than if you simply tugged upward on the back-of-the-head string.

To take full advantage of this effect, give your puppet a rope or cloth neck. When you carve or model the head make sure to leave out the neck. Instead, leave a small hole where the rope or cloth neck can be glued and/or stapled into place. Then find a length of thick but extremely supple rope (if you can't find

Fig. 4-16. A string neck allows for mobility and expression.

any, sew a tube out of soft cloth; this will do equally well). Use staples and glue to fix the rope to the underside of the head, where the puppet's neck ought to be; then string the puppet up normally, with shoulder strings.

Your rope-necked puppet will have an extremely mobile and expressive head. This is an excellent way to recreate the stooped upper body of an old man or woman, or the hunched shoulders of a villain hatching a sneaky plan (FIG. 4-16). Rope necks are not only for codgers and bad guys. Virtually any character type can benefit from the subtlety of expression that a rope neck permits (FIG. 4-17).

ELBOW STRINGS, AND OTHER HIGH TECHNOLOGY

If you have a moment to spare, try the following experiment. Tie a length of thread to one end of a pencil, and try to control the angle and position of the

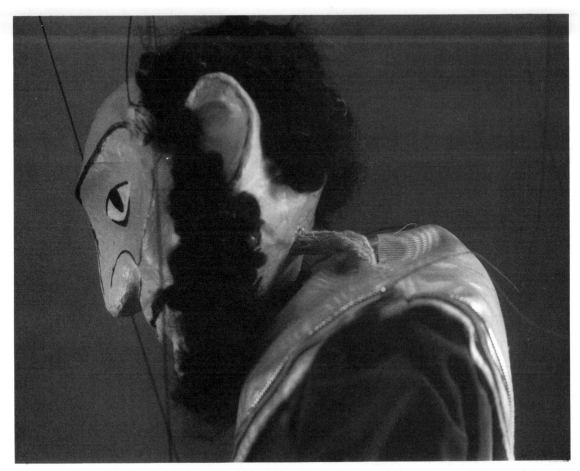

Fig. 4-17. A rope neck gives a puppet a particularly mobile and expressive head. (Photograph by Jano Salinas.)

pencil by moving the thread up, down, and around. Unless the laws of physics have changed since the last time I tried this, you should find that your control is quite limited. The pencil will simply hang, with one end down and the other end up and the whole thing twirling about uncontrollably. Now tie a second length of thread to the *other* end of the pencil, making a sort of trapeze. By holding the two threads you can guide the movement of the pencil in all directions. You can tilt it up or down or swivel it from side to side. You have complete control.

Now that we've paid homage to the marvels of natural science, we can extend the Pencil Principle to the business of controlling a puppet's arms. By running a continuous string from one elbow to the other, you can dramatically improve your puppet's manual coordination (FIG. 4-18). Tie the string to a screw eye mounted on the puppet's upper arm, a little above the elbow joint (FIG. 4-19). The elbow string should run outside the hand string (FIG. 4-20). A good way to keep everything in place is to put a "spreader" crosspiece on the front of the marionette control. In FIG. 4-21, the strings (a) run to the elbows while strings (b) run to the hands.

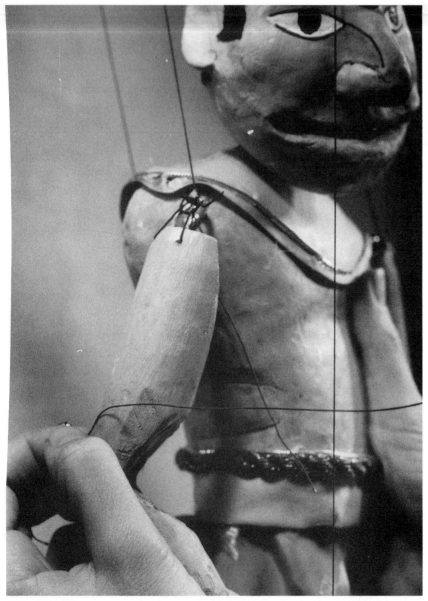

Fig. 4-18. Elbow strings give the puppeteer more control over the marionette's arms. (Photograph by Jano Salinas.)

You can use the same stringing arrangement to add a set of wrist strings, although most puppets function very well without them. (Obviously, these should only be added if the marionette has jointed wrists.) Attach the string to a screw eye mounted on the forearm, a little above the wrist.

A dancer or a sorceror might require special arm or hand movements. Try switching the strings around, so that the continuous string on the left hand runs

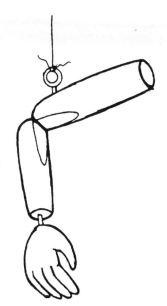

Fig. 4-19. This string allows the puppet arm control.

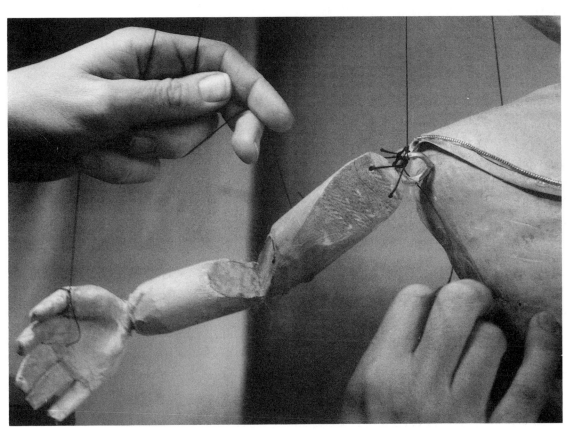

Fig. 4-20. A puppet's arm is tied to his body with strong nylon fishing line (Photograph by Jano Salinas.)

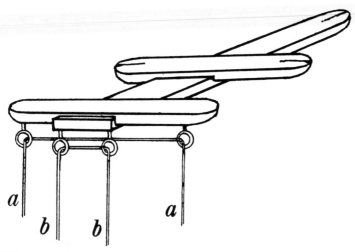

Fig. 4-21. A spreader on the crosspiece keeps the strings in place.

to the screw eye on the right wrist or elbow—and vice versa. As you pull down on the left hand string, the right elbow (or wrist) will go up. As you pull up on the left elbow (or wrist) string, the right hand will drop. The effect, at once bizarre and graceful, is perfect for exotic characters.

A FEW MORE OF MY FAVORITE STRINGS

Strings can be used to correct defects in the way the puppet is built. If your marionette has an oddly shaped head, he might have trouble looking up. Long-faced or big-chinned puppets are especially susceptible to this embarrassment. To correct it, simply run a string from the tip of the nose to the centerpiece of the control (FIG. 4-22).

Flying is easy for a marionette (so easy that it often happens by mistake). Just raise the control and you have lift off. However, if you want the puppet to fly horizontally—Superman style—you must run strings from the back of his ankles to the back end of the control. Ankle strings can also be used to make the puppet swim, or perform handstands (FIG. 4-23).

Getting the audience to applaud is simple; getting the *puppets* to clap their hands is slightly harder. With a normal stringing arrangement, you can move the puppet's hands together by pulling in on the continuous hand string. But if you want a puppet's hands to come together suddenly and decisively you should equip him with a special hand-clapping string. This string runs through a hole on the palm of one hand and is securely fastened to the palm of the other (FIG. 4-24). The same principle can be used to bring various objects into the puppet's hand, or to bring the hands up to the face.

Experiment with other strings. A chin string permits the puppet to cock his head sharply to one side. A belly string lets him arch his back, or "crabwalk," belly up, on his hands and feet. There are hundreds of other possibilities, and

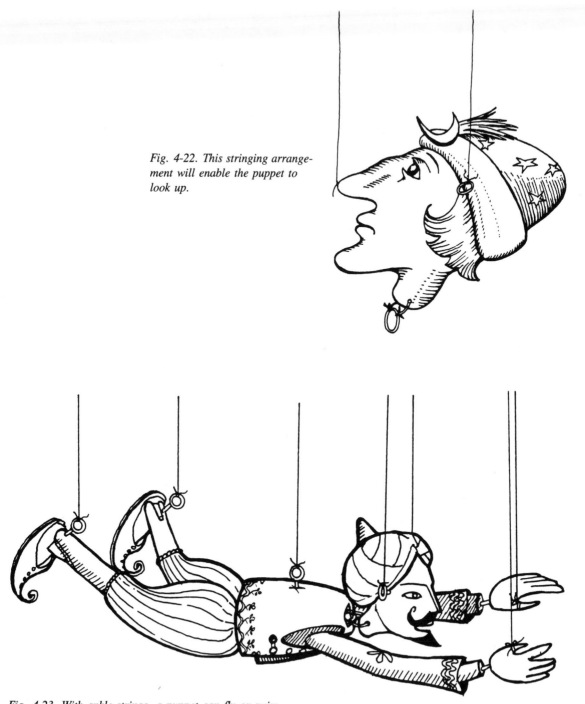

Fig. 4-22. This stringing arrangement will enable the puppet to look up.

Fig. 4-23. With ankle strings, a puppet can fly or swim.

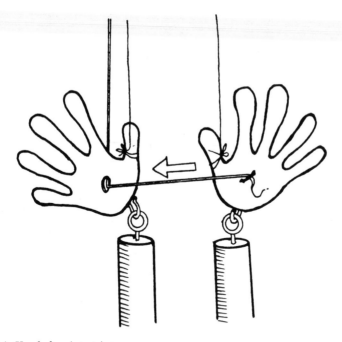

Fig. 4-24. Hand-clapping strings.

I'll describe some of them in the sections on stunt puppetry in Chapter VI, and special effects in Chapter VIII.

Now that you've gotten the hang of strings, I am sorry to report that you will have to untie most of them. It's time to get your puppet into costume, and the strings must come off before the threads go on. So loosen his ties, detach the control, and read on.

V

Costumes, Hats, and Wigs

Above all . . . let the marionettes remind us that the art of the theatre should be beautiful first and then indeed what you will afterwards.

Arthur Symons (1902)

THE TYPICAL PUPPETEER (IF THERE IS SUCH A THING) IS AN INVETERATE PACK rat and garbage picker, scuttling between junk shops and back alleys, stuffing his satchel with remnants of fabric and wood. As a puppeteer-to-be, you might as well resign yourself to it. From the moment you embark upon a production, you will look at trash with new eyes. Objects that you once happily discarded—bath mats, foam rubber and bits of frayed twine—will begin to seem fabulously valuable. In fact, you will develop a whole new perspective on the world around you. While others are enjoying a fine wine, you will be wondering how you can use the corks. While others are admiring a new silk tie, you will secretly reflect that it would make a perfect cloak lining for the Caliph of Bagdhad.

When it comes time to costume your puppets, this mania is sure to reach fever pitch. It is possible to *buy* all the fabrics and ornaments you will need to clothe your troupe; but if you do so you will miss out on one of the greatest pleasures that puppetry affords, that of giving new life to forgotten objects and materials. Puppet makers collect rags and buttons as others do stamps or butterflies. I recommend that you start a rag bag of your own. You should have no trouble finding things to fill it with.

Almost anything can be useful, from your torn flannel pajamas to your brand new leopard-skin pillbox hat. Be on the lookout for small pieces of the more sumptuous or unusual fabrics, such as metallic satins or rich brocades. A fabric shop might be willing to give you their obsolete sample books. These only contain one small patch of each type of cloth, but this is enough for many purposes (FIG. 5-1). Puppets take a small size, after all. It might even be worth your while to buy old clothing from yard sales and secondhand stores. A well-used evening gown that costs you 75¢ might be decorated with several dollars worth of beads, buttons, and fancy trim.

Bear in mind that any fabric will look very different on a puppet than on a human being. The most tawdry and eccentric materials can look elegant and tasteful on a puppet, and expensive finery can look surprisingly dull. The important thing is to see your old materials in new ways. The toe of a worn-out sock can make a stylish wool hat; a cheap lamé handbag can be transmuted, by the alchemy of the imagination, into Cinderalla's gown. It's all up to you.

When you set out to design clothes for a string marionette, your first consideration is freedom of movement. The puppet's garments must interfere as

Fig. 5-1. Instead of painting props and scenery, you can cover surfaces with pieces of colored cloth. On cloth backgrounds, you might wish to sew the fabric into place. In most cases you can apply it with white glue. (Photograph by Jano Salinas.)

little as possible with limbs and strings. You might be surprised at how easy it is to go wrong. If the puppet's collar is too high his head won't turn properly. If the cloth around his shoulders or knees is too heavy he will suffer from stiff joints. If his jacket is studded with sequins or beads they might snag his strings or, worse, the strings of other puppets onstage. When this happens during a show it can be acutely embarrassing to the puppeteer.

I remember one performance where the good guy and the villain became tangled up together and waltzed through the final minutes of the scene, entwined in what appeared to be a warm and loving embrace. At such moments you will wish you had designed the puppets costumes with the prevention of tangles uppermost in your mind.

Some types of cloth are more appropriate than others. A common fault, even among professional puppeteers, is the use of fabrics that don't "flow." When used in small pieces, a heavy, tightly woven cloth will tend to hang badly. A cloak or dress cut from such cloth will stick out in all the wrong places, reminding the audience that the creature that stands before them is only 16 inches tall. For this reason, puppets should generally be dressed in lightweight fabrics, or in cloth with very little "body." You can get away with heavier cloth if you select a synthetic knit that hangs in attractive folds. A further advantage of knits is they tend not to unravel, so you might be able to get away without hemming your puppet's garment. If you are using woven cloth, stick to light silks and cottons.

In choosing a fabric, your second consideration is how it will appear to the audience. When using patterned cloth, remember that the pattern should be in proportion to the size of the marionette. A floral print showing lush masses of roses will probably look strange on the puppet's tiny body. There might be room for only half a bouquet, which might, in any case, be mistaken for a splotch of spaghetti sauce. Think about how the cloth will appear from a distance. A pattern of tiny stars might look like polka dots from afar, and even solid colors could undergo some changes. Some fabrics will look rather drab under the stage lights. Others will positively glow. (Silks often reflect a lot of light without creating any glare, which makes them perfect for puppet theatre).

As you go about collecting cloth, keep an eye out for pieces of fringe, lace, ribbon, braid, and other decorative odds and ends. All sorts of ornaments can be sewn to the costume or even stuck on with glue. These are particularly useful for hiding seams and ragged edges. A length of ribbon glued along the fringe of a garment can eliminate the need to sew a proper hemline. Inventive use of piping or embroidery strips can save you a lot of sewing. In fact, why bother sewing at all? Nail the puppet's shirt right to his chest and then conceal the grisly deed beneath layers of ruffles and lace. However, don't go overboard with fancywork. You are making a marionette, not a gingerbread man. Your puppet should not look decorated, but rather, dressed. In fact, he should look as if he dressed himself.

CLOTHES MAKE THE PUPPET

A marionette's clothes reveal his position in puppet society. The face and body tell you about his personality, but clothing reveals his social status, his job, his role, in short his public self. Ask ten people to draw a king and you will be shown ten different faces and facial expressions, but each one will be wearing a crown. Never mind that a real king is more likely to be seen in a yachting cap—the stereotypes are extremely durable.

From a very young age we are encouraged to identify people by their paraphernalia. Open a child's book and you'll see what I mean. Most show a simplified version of the world, in which farmers wear overalls, scientists wear spectacles, and witches for some reason flit about with black traffic cones on their heads. The list of such standard devices is virtually endless. In designing costumes you don't have to resort to these devices, but neither can you afford to completely ignore them. If you don't give your chef an apron and a puffy white hat, you might need to explain in words that he is a chef. And in a puppet show, words can be powerfully soporific.

Clothing immediately locates the play in space and time. If the characters strut onstage in knee breeches and powdered wigs, the audience knows right away that they are in eighteenth century Europe. It is up to the puppeteer to know how people might have dressed in, say, Mozart's Vienna. But if you've never worn a powdered wig, how can you design one that looks right?

To convey a strong sense of time and place, you will probably need to do a bit of research. Your local library is your best resource here, and getting what you need from it can be a lot of fun. Let's say you are staging a story from *The Thousand and One Nights*. Over the years you've probably seen hundreds of representations of "Arabian" characters, in films, picture books, and cartoons. You're probably quite familiar with what usually passes for Arabian dress: pointy shoes, turbans, baggy trousers, and veils of gauze. You could probably base your costumes entirely on picture book versions, but why not take your research further? Why not have a look at how people actually dressed at the time the stories were collected? You could browse through collections of Persian illuminations or of miniature paintings from the Ottoman Turkish empire. The more you bring to your show the more people will get from it (FIG. 5-2).

No matter what culture or historical period you are portraying, you can probably find plenty of paintings or drawings to base costumes on. For a show based on an Amerindian legend, you would do well to examine reproductions of native art and artifacts. For a show set in ancient Egypt, you could adapt costumes from Egyptian tomb frescoes, showing scenes from everyday life (FIG. 5-3).

Even if your puppet play is an outright fantasy, set at no particular date or place, it would be worth your while to leaf through a history of costume. You might find that the reality of fashion history is far, far stranger than any fantasy you could concoct. In the eighteenth century, for instance, some women wore dresses that made them considerably wider than they were tall. A skirt like the one that graced the wedding costume of Sweden's Queen Sophia Magdalena required an elaborate framework of iron ribs and braces, turning the wearer into a sort of gigantic spaghetti-strainer (FIG. 5-4). This sort of excess is far from rare in the history of fashion. So don't be reluctant to use history to supplement your own imagination.

Fig. 5-2. Puppets dressed in the style of the Ottoman Turks.

91

Fig. 5-3. Puppets modeled after Egyptian frescoes.

MAKING THE CLOTHES

The good news for nonsewers is that, for the marionettes' clothing, you usually don't have to stitch the seams. In most cases, you can get away with just tacking them. Of course if you are the obssessive type you can hem every edge and double stitch each seam and create perfect little replicas of real garments for your puppets to wear. Unfortunately, your painstaking labor will be wasted because nobody in the audience will ever know, or care, that you have done it.

You will probably not be able to eliminate sewing entirely. It will still be necessary to do some work with needle and thread. But wherever possible, make things easy on yourself: use glue.

Fig. 5-4. The wedding dress of Queen Sophia Magdalena of Sweden, 1766.

Several types of glue are appropriate for attaching puppet clothing. If you are in a hurry, you will find it very useful to use a glue gun, an electrical appliance about the size of a large soldering gun. The user inserts hard sticks of a special type of glue in the back end of the gun. An internal heating element melts the sticks down and the tip of the gun emits a thin stream of hot, molten glue. This cools very quickly, providing an instant bond. The glue is not strong enough for major construction projects, but it is perfect for small jobs, such as attaching the shirt to a puppet's back.

If you don't have a glue gun, you can make do with other adhesives, such as ordinary white glue. The only disadvantage of white glue is that it will soak through some types of cloth, marring the surface. Obviously, this is not a problem when the joint is to be covered up with a strip of braid or trim.

Finally, sewing supply stores often carry special glues that are meant to be used with cloth. These are designed not to soak through the fabric. Also, the glues themselves are quite flexible, so they may be used on loose, hanging cloth without losing their adhesive properties. Note: (Glue gun sticks are quite inflexible and are appropriate only for applying cloth directly to rigid surfaces such as the puppet's body.)

There is no room in this chapter to describe all the kinds of clothing it is possible to make. Instead I will illustrate a few useful techniques and provide diagrams of several all-purpose garments.

Fig. 5-5. A plain tunic.

Tunic

The tunic in FIG. 5-5 can be shortened to make a shirt or lengthened to make a floor-length robe. It is basically a rectangular piece of cloth folded once at the shoulders (FIG. 5-6).

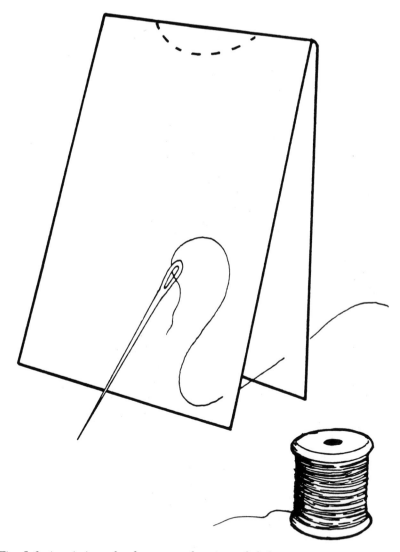

Fig. 5-6. A tunic is made of a rectangular piece of cloth.

Cut a hole for the neck and sew (or glue) the sides (FIG. 5-7). Turn the whole tunic inside out when you are done, so that the seams don't show. Most fabrics are quite different on one side than on the other, so remember to arrange the cloth so that the good side will be on the outside when the tunic is turned inside out. Also follow the correct "direction" of the cloth.

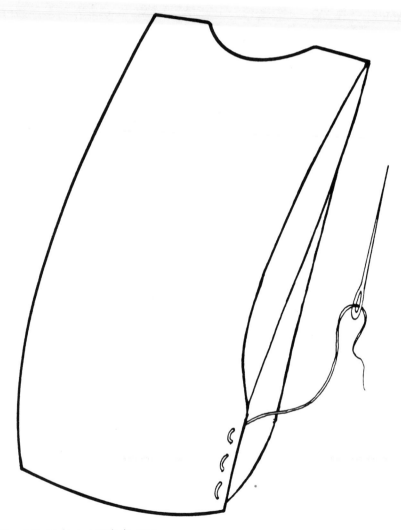

Fig. 5-7. Making a tunic is easy.

If you are using a fine synthetic knit, there is no need to hem the lower edge. In fact, a hem will only stiffen the cloth, so that it does not hang well. If you are using a woven cloth, you will probably have to hem it or else glue a strip of ribbon or braid along the hemline to prevent it from unravelling and to hide the ragged edge.

The sleeves of this tunic are made separately. The sleeve is basically a tube of cloth, with a single seam running up one side. Glue or sew this seam, as you prefer. If possible, use the selvage of the fabric for the bottom of the cuff. Again, this will save you from having to make a hem. Either way, be sure to turn the tube inside out after you have completed the sleeve. Do the same for all tubular shapes. Notice that the sleeves are not actually attached to the rest of the tunic, but are glued directly to the wood of the puppet's shoulder, encircling the screw eye of the shoulder joint. This not only saves you some sewing, it also ensures that the marionette will have complete freedom of movement in the upper arms (FIG. 5-8).

You can make the sleeves and the tunic out of different types of cloth, which creates the impression that the puppet has a shirt on under his jacket. The tunic can also be shortened a bit so that it becomes a sleeveless vest (FIG. 5-9).

Sleeves can be varied according to the type of costume you are making. If you want the puppet to have puffy sleeves, then make a tapered tube, much wider at the shoulder than at the wrist (FIG. 5-10). Now "gather" the shoulder cloth by running a thread around the wide end of the tube and then pulling the thread tight. This pulls the fabric in, rather like the drawstring of a cloth bag. Attach the sleeve in the normal way. You can create different types of sleeves simply by varying the shape of the cloth with which you make the tube. Cut the cuff

Fig. 5-8. The sleeves are separate from the rest of the tunic, allowing freedom of movement.

Fig. 5-9. The vest: a variation of the tunic.

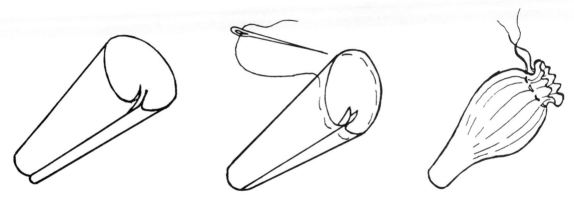

Fig. 5-10. Sleeves can be made to suit the costume.

very wide to make a type of long, hanging sleeve that was popular during the Middle Ages, or gather it in ruffles for a French musketeer.

Collar

The best marionette neck joint is one that permits the head to move freely in all directions. The kind of neck joint we described in Chapter III meets this criterion very well. Unfortunately, it does not look particularly natural. In fact, if you don't do something to conceal the neck it will seem as if the puppet's head is floating above its shoulders. One way to hide the attachment is to sink the screw eye to which the neck is tied inside a small hole in the wood of the marionette's shoulders. However, if the hole in the wood is deep enough to hide the gap between neck and shoulders, it will almost certainly affect the movement of the head. It is much better to design clothes that will cover the neck joint. There are very few cases where this is not possible. Even a puppet that is naked from the waist up might be given a neck ornament or cowl.

In most cases you will want to add a collar of some type to a shirt or jacket. One of the easiest is the traditional Punch-style collar, which you can make by gathering one side of a long strip of cloth. The cloth should be relatively stiff so that it forms definite folds (FIG. 5-11).

Floppy ruffles are all very well if your puppet is a clown. But suppose he or she is a business executive. To make a true, tailored collar you will need to stiffen the cloth so that it retains its shape while it is cut and worked. One way to do this is to glue another layer of cloth to the fabric you are using for the collar. Soak the two layers in white glue diluted with a little bit of water. When the cloth is dry it will be quite stiff. It is then possible to cut and shape the cloth without sewing hems. You can get the same effect by using a special iron-on interfacing material, which can be found at a fabric and sewing supply shop (FIG. 5-12).

This technique can be adapted for many costume features, such as contoured shoulders, cuffs, belts and lapels. It is also a good way to shape hats and bonnets.

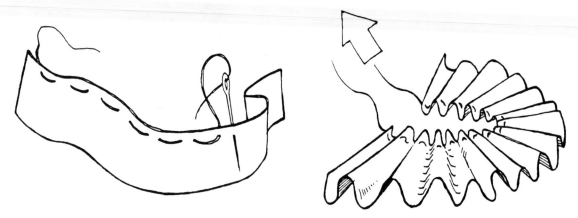

Fig. 5-11. Collars hide the neck attachment.

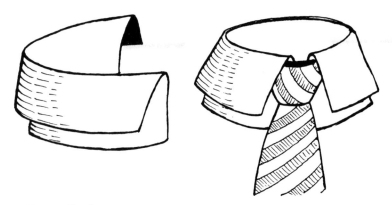

Fig. 5-12. A stiff collar.

Breeches

Trousers will be very easy to make, provided your puppet's jacket or tunic is long enough. If the puppet's hips are hidden by the hem of his jacket, there's no need to make the upper portion of the marionette's breeches. Just sew two tubes of cloth and glue them around the upper thigh. Taper the tubes so that they are quite wide at hips and knees. Check to see that knees and hips still move freely (FIG. 5-13).

Try to avoid making a full pair of breeches. If you make them loose enough to allow full movement of the legs, they will probably look baggy. And if you make them tight enough to be stylish, they will reduce mobility. However, if the puppet's costume absolutely requires that hips be exposed, get out needle and thread and make a full pair of pants. Select a very supple fabric and make two tapered tubes, leaving plenty of free cloth at the top so that the two leg tubes can be joined at the waist (FIG. 5-14).

You can probably get away with gluing the waist and hips of the trousers directly to the puppet's wooden pelvis. You can sew the upper portion of the

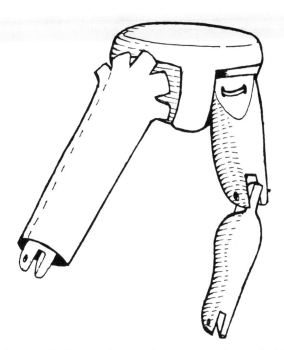

Fig. 5-13. If the puppet's hips aren't exposed, trousers can be attached directly to legs.

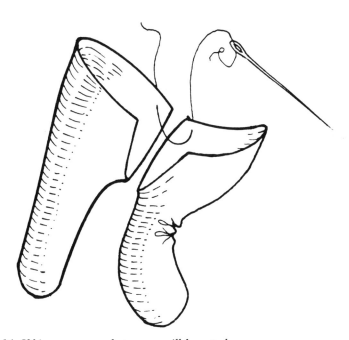

Fig. 5-14. If hips are exposed, trousers will have to be sewn.

leg tubes together (although you should be able to manage with glue). Don't attempt to join the two leg tubes together *under* the crotch area. This will only interfere with the leg movements.

Skirts

For those who are not skilled with a needle and thread, a basic skirt can be as simple as a piece of cloth sewn into a tube and gathered at the waist. This will give a full skirt that will bell out in folds. The larger the tube, the fuller the skirt. If you prefer a close-fitting garment, without folds or pleats, start with a narrower semicircular shape, as in FIG. 5-15. A narrower semicircle will give a tighter skirt.

Capes are made in roughly the same way as skirts. A small cape, like Superman's may be cut from any kind of cloth, but a large cape, like Dracula's, should be made of an extremely light fabric. If it covers the puppet's shoulders, it will also cover the upper part of the arms, making them heavy and awkward.

WIGS

The puppets have been bald since Chapter II. Now it is time to give them wigs. Most of what we've already said about costumes applies also to hairstyles. The puppet's coiffure should be designed to complement the design of the costume.

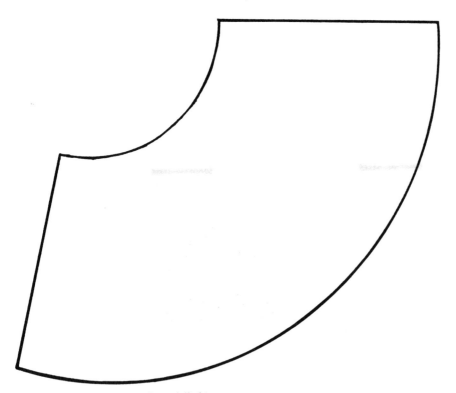

Fig. 5-15. An easy pattern for a full skirt.

However, the material you use to make the hair itself will depend more on the style of the show and on the character of the individual puppet.

Perhaps the worst material for making hair is hair. If you had planned to snip a few ringlets from your own coiffure, be advised that real human hair is very hard to transplant and probably won't look good on your puppet anyway. The difficulty comes from the fact that locks of hair must be glued flat to the puppets scalp, so that every single hair is anchored in the glue. Even if you succeed in getting the hairs in place without burying the top of the puppet's head under enormous blobs of glue, you will probably have to settle for a very wild and scruffy hairstyle. If that suits your purposes, fine. Find somebody with the right kind of hair—shave the sheepdog, if necessary—and glue your clippings to the bare papier-mâché scalp, using any transparent adhesive.

However, there are many good alternatives to real hair. As I mentioned in Chapter II, it is possible to model the hair out of papier-mâché at the same time as you do the head itself. Then you have only to paint the hair and add any other ornamentation—a net, a string of pearls—to complete the effect. You can also add a papier-mâché hairstyle after the head has been made. A good way to do this is to soak strips of Kleenex or paper towel in a very thick flour paste. Add these to the puppet's head, one strip at a time. If you make the strips thick enough they can even be braided, or laid out in tight curls.

Many kinds of string, yarn, and decorative piping are good for puppet hair. Ordinary yarn tends to make rather ordinary-looking hair. But these days there are many exotic kinds to choose from. Some shops carry specialty yarns with all sorts of fascinating lumps and fibers twisted into them. A visit to a well-stocked knitting and fabric store will suggest things to you. Keep in mind that many kinds of yarn and twine can be altered. Unravelled strands of yarn sometimes fall in delicate ringlets, and frayed jute makes a splendid mane for a wildman. Also, you can treat yarn with glue, just as you would papier-mâché. For example, try coiling a length of wool yarn around a tubular object, such as a pencil. Soak the yarn in white glue. When the glue is dry, remove the pencil. You will be left with a lock of curly marionette hair. The curl won't lose its shape—it's a sort of puppet permanent.

When scavenging hair, you should keep an eye out for fibers that are already attached to a backing of some sort. Some types of shag rug might be appropriate, or even ordinary broadloom if your puppet is supposed to be wearing a brush cut (FIG. 5-16).

The fur of some animals may create just the effect you want. You can make woolly curls by applying small patches of sheepskin (FIG. 5-17). Use patches of goatskin to make the scraggly hair and whiskers of a miser, or use white rabbit fur for the downy ear tufts of a professor. The possibilities are virtually limitless. A kindly puppet can wear plumes clipped from a feather duster, and a nasty one can sport a coiffure of 2-inch nails. Cloth hair is good for almost any style of puppet. Felt or velvet can be cut into strips (FIG. 5-18), or applied in patches (FIG. 5-19).

Fig. 5-16. Pieces of rug may be used for certain types of hairstyles.

Fig. 5-17. Sheepskin works well for curly hairdos.

I won't attempt a complete list of suitable materials. Straw, scouring pads, coconut husk are all examples. Be alert to all the hairy, fibrous, twiny stuff that surrounds us and you won't lack the material to make a wig.

HATS

If you have carried out the instructions given earlier in this book, you are already a seamstress, a carpenter, a sculptor, and a wigmaker. However, you will be

104

Fig. 5-18. Cloth such as felt or velvet can be cut in strips to use as hair.

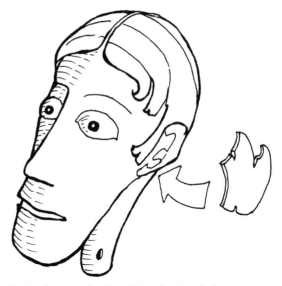

Fig. 5-19. Flat hairstyles can also be achieved using cloth.

able to call yourself a puppeteer only when you have mastered *all* the trades, because puppetry recapitulates every other human activity in miniature. It is not for specialists. Puppeteers, as the saying goes, must wear many hats: one of those hats is that of the "hatter." Not every puppet needs one, but every puppeteer must know how to make one.

Papier-mâché, the all-purpose medium, is also ideal for hatting. The trick to making a good hat out of paper is selecting the right mold to build it around. An upturned glass or small bowl will sometimes do. If your hat is of a particularly complicated style, you might want to mold it in plasticine first. The technique

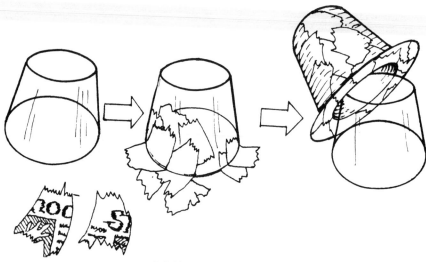

Fig. 5-20. Forming a papier-mâché hat.

is exactly the same as for making heads, except that you will not have to slice the papier-mâché in two in order to remove it from the mold. No matter what you use as a hat form, give it a good slathering of Vaseline before applying the papier-mâché (FIG. 5-20).

There are other ways to make hats. One excellent method is to carve a shape out of foam rubber and then cover it with a layer of cloth. Do the carving with an ordinary pair of scissors, the larger the better. If you plan to do a lot of foam-cutting, reserve a special pair of shears for the job, because foam dulls scissors very quickly (FIG. 5-21).

When you have the shape you want, select a knit fabric with a certain amount of stretch to it, and apply it the surface of the foam. Use a glue gun or contact cement to attach the cloth (white glue will not adhere to foam rubber). Compress the foam as you work, so that the cloth will be tight (FIG. 5-22).

Finally, add feathers, embroidery, or decorative trim. Incidentally, if you cannot find appropriate decorations, you can design your own, drawing patterns on the surface of the cloth with glue from a glue gun. This technique is not just for hats: it permits you to apply raised ornamentation to any surface. Simply draw the motif with strings of molten glue. When the design has hardened, paint the glue with an opague acrylic or oil-based paint. This is especially useful for imitating fancy metalwork on shields and helmets.

You can also assemble hats and bonnets entirely from cloth. This scarf requires little explanation (FIG. 5-23).

FIGURE 5-24 illustrates a Georgian bonnet, made by gathering a circular piece of cloth. Do the gathering with a piece of colorful ribbon or yarn.

You can combine plain cloth with cardboard or iron-on interfacing to create a number of different styles. Add a strip of stiffened fabric to the bottom of the Georgian bonnet to make a chef's hat (FIG. 5-25).

106

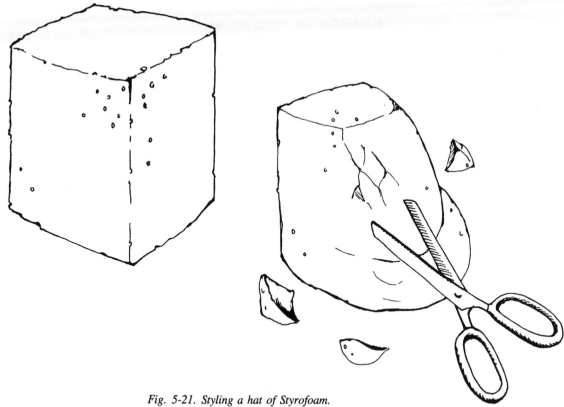

Fig. 5-21. Styling a hat of Styrofoam.

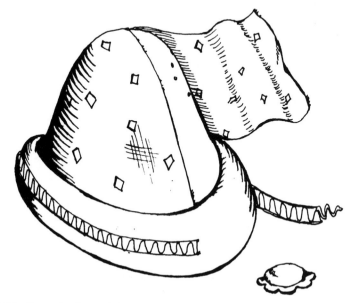

Fig. 5-22. Cover the form of the hat with fabric.

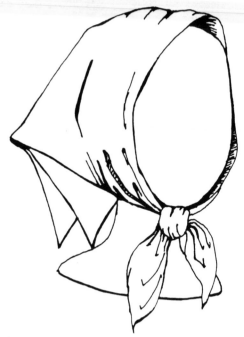

Fig. 5-23. A scarf for a puppet.

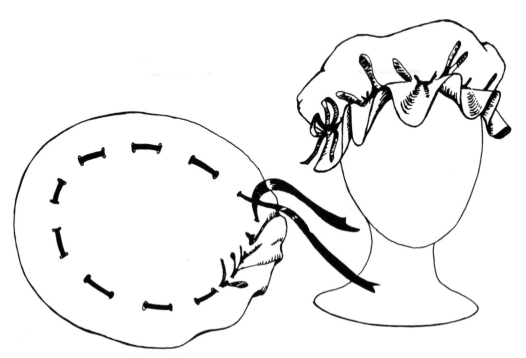

Fig. 5-24. A bonnet can be made from a circular piece of cloth.

108

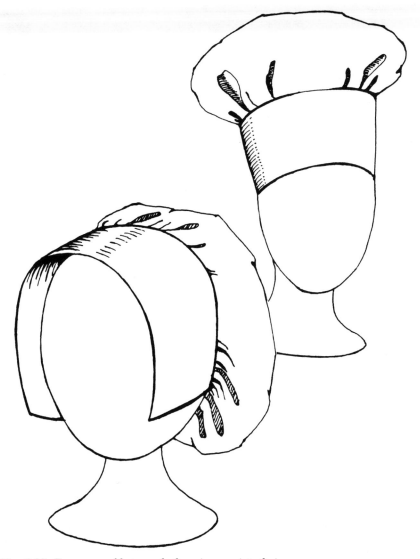

Fig. 5-25. Two types of hats made from iron-on interfacing.

Some hats might require a mixture of techniques. The basic shape of a top hat can be arrived at with cardboard and cloth, but you might wish to reinforce the cardboard under-structure with papier-mâché (FIG. 5-26). The same goes for the standard tricorn hat. Although it looks quite difficult, the shape is easy to make using a basic hat form with a rounded crown and a floppy brim (FIG. 5-27).

Various household objects such as tuna cans or the lid to a jar of mayonnaise can be incorporated into the hat itself. Here is a pillbox hat that is made of pillbox (FIG. 5-28).

Fig. 5-26. Cardboard covered with cloth can make a variety of hats.

In elementary school you might have decorated bottles with shell macaroni and painted them gold or silver. Using the same principle, you can assemble some rather elaborate crowns or helmets. Use epoxy to cement various decorative objects—buttons, bottlecaps, medicine containers—around a central structure such as a yogurt dish or an upturned tea sieve. When the objects are all painted the same color or covered with the same material, they will suddenly look as if they belong together (FIG. 5-29).

Your puppet is now clothed wigged, hatted, and ready to meet the world. You are faced with a choice. You can stop here, nail the puppet over the fireplace, sink back into an overstuffed chair, and contemplate your handiwork—or you can go on to stage a show. I hope that, having come this far, you'll keep going. The remaining portion of this book is devoted to stage craft, special effects, and trick puppetry.

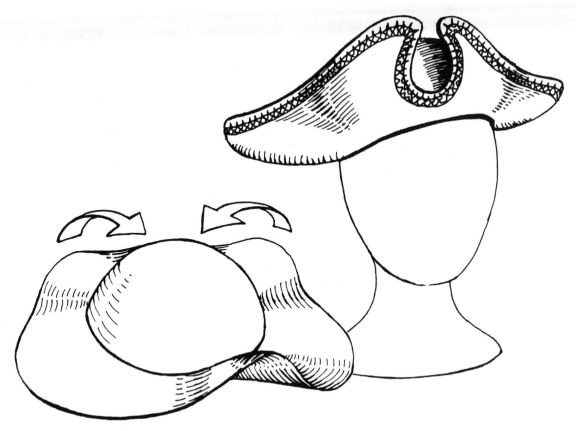

Fig. 5-27. A tricorn hat is easy to make.

Fig. 5-28. A pillbox makes a pillbox hat.

Fig. 5-29. *Household objects can be used to make elaborate hats.*

VI

Stunt Puppets

Where is the thread now? Off again!
The old trick!

"Two in the Campagna"
Robert Browning

I WAS GOING TO START THIS CHAPTER BY SAYING THAT PUPPETS CAN DO ANY-thing. But let's not lose our grip on reality. The fact is, there are things puppets will never do, but there are no limits to what puppets can *seem* to do. Nevertheless, there are certain tasks that are too dangerous or difficult for the average marionette; such tasks call for a specialist, a marionette with a particular skill. It's the same way in the movie business. A film screenplay might contain directions that the average actor just isn't equipped to handle, so the director calls in a stunt man for those scenes. Stunt experts can do certain things very well, such as drive cement trucks off cliffs, or hang by the heels from runaway stallions, or convincingly blast themselves to smithereens. But they are not, as a rule, particularly versatile. They confine themselves to the exotic and dangerous things that no sane person would attempt, and leave the acting to the actors.

Such is the case with stunt puppets. They are usually designed to do one or two things well, but they are limited to those things. With special stringing, you can make a stunt puppet perform actions that no human being would attempt, but that usually means the puppet can't do normal actions. A juggler generally can't do much except juggle, and an acrobat who can spin cartwheels up and down the stage might find walking in a straight line nearly impossible. Stunt puppets can add a lot to a show, as long as you understand their limitations. As a rule, the more spectacular the stunt, the less versatile the puppet.

The most convenient way to use a stunt puppet is to bring it on to perform its tricks, then usher it offstage as quickly as possible. Unfortunately, this makes it difficult to incorporate a stunt puppet into the storyline. Unless your play is set in a circus, it is hard to justify interrupting the narrative for a tumbling display or tightrope act. If it comes to a choice between maintaining narrative continuity and staging a neat trick, choose continuity. Nothing can replace the dramatic energy that develops as an exciting story unfolds.

One way to incorporate stunts into the show without interfering with story development is to have the main characters of the show do the stunts. How is this possible, in light of what I've already said about specialization? Make two puppets. A look-alike puppet can stand in for the main character when he or she is required to do something difficult. The double must be dressed exactly like the main puppet and must have exactly the same facial features. If possible, cast the double's face from the same mold as the original. Use a plaster mold as described in Chapter II to cast as many papier-mâché duplicates as you require.

In some situations you will be able to do an entire scene with the stand-in More often, you'll have to find an excuse for getting the main puppet offstage so you can replace him or her with the duplicate. This need not create an awkward moment onstage. Puppets enter and exit all the time, so that will not surprise your audience. Simply adjust the action and dialogue of the scene so that it seems normal for the puppet to exit, then return with his juggling balls or weightlifting equipment.

Some traditional stunt puppets, such as the Grand Turk and the three-headed Scaramouche, are very difficult to incorporate into a story. These are best used in a marionette circus or variety show. I have included several puppets of this type in the following pages because they are traditional, and because they illustrate techniques that you can adapt for other purposes.

THE DISJOINTING SKELETON

The Disjointing Skeleton, one of the oldest of the traditional trick puppets, has existed in one form or another for 200 years (FIG. 6-1). The custom of personifying Death as a skeleton is even older. An indispensable character in the morality theater of the Middle Ages, Death would appear suddenly in the middle of a comic religious drama to put an end to a sinner's career or frighten him into changing his ways. The tradition of the disjointing skeleton might have originated in theatre of this kind. He is essentially a dancing puppet, so his beginnings are probably connected with the long tradition of the Dance of Death, in which the reaper would lead a troupe of citizens from every social class to their graves, holding hands and dancing all the way. You might have seen portrayals of this in medieval art, or in the clockwork figures that adorn the great Gothic timepieces in European cathedrals and town squares.

At first, the disjointing skeleton seems much like any other puppet. He does have a few limitations. He can't bend over or tilt his head forward; he's rather

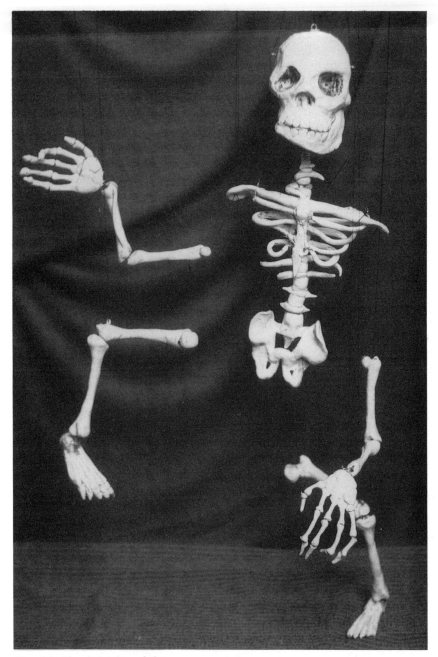

Fig. 6-1. The disjointing skeleton.

stiff, which is understandable, considering his circumstances. In spite of this he is a very competent dancer, and can shake and rattle with the best of them. However, he has one trick that really sets him apart: he falls to pieces. His arms and legs detach themselves from his body and his head pops off. All of his separate parts hover in the air for one horrible instant, then everything snaps back into place and he resumes his grisly dance. He repeats this several times, and each time his dance grows more wild and frenzied. Finally he crashes to the floor in a jumbled heap of ribs and vertebrae. The bones lie quiet for a moment, then begin to twitch and shift. The skeleton pulls himself together, and dances off stage.

Though he looks terribly complicated, the skeleton is not too difficult to make and use. Traditionally he is carved out of wood. Model the head—or skull, rather—in papier-mâché. (Give him a hinged jaw if you want to make him particularly hideous). Make papier-mâché hands and feet at the same time. Apply the papier-mâché to a wire frame, taking care not to let the fingers or toes get too thick. Create segments in the fingers and toes to suggest that they are jointed.

Carve the limbs out of ½- or ¾-inch dowelling. Leave the joints quite thick, but shave the rest down to a bone-like slenderness. Don't try for too much anatomical detail; there are dozens of large bones in the human body but nobody will notice if you only include the very largest of them. The knee and elbow joints could be made of interlocking screw eyes. It doesn't matter if the arms and legs move somewhat haphazardly; this will only add to the bizarre effect. Nevertheless, you might prefer to make proper tongue-and-groove joints for the arms and legs. If you have the patience, by all means do it. Remember, however, that this will mean making the joints somewhat thicker than they would otherwise have to be.

Carve the pelvis out of a block of softwood or, if you prefer, assemble it out of very thin plywood. Cut the ribs from the same kind of plywood. Cut the crescent-shaped ribs with a scroll saw. The ribs should decrease in size from the shoulders to the hips. Cut slices from a piece of dowelling to make vertebrae. Drill holes through the ribs and vertebrae. Glue everything together and run a thin metal rod or wire through the holes to keep the segments in line (FIG. 6-2).

Paint the finished skeleton with a fluorescent white paint, using blue-grey shadows in the hollows of his bones. The fluorescent paint will give the skeleton's bones an unearthly radiance. To fully exploit this effect, perform the dance under black light. Dim the overhead floods and train a strong ultraviolet light on the skeleton. An incandescent black light will not provide enough illumination to create a suitably eerie ambience, so use a fluorescent tube.

The disjointing skeleton is traditionally made of wood, but I suggest you try making one out of a product which is sold under the name "Fimo". Fimo, which is available at art stores and hobby shops, is a modeling medium that can be shaped like plasticine. When it is baked for 10 or 15 minutes in an ordinary home oven, it becomes a hard plastic, which is very durable but retains a certain amount of flexibility.

Start with a length of wire. Bend a small loop in each end, then mold the Fimo around the wire (FIG. 6-3). Make loops in a second length of wire. Hook this wire to the first and apply Fimo (FIG. 6-4).

Make all four limbs in this way, and use the same basic technique to make hands and feet. Make sure to loop the wire of the wrists and ankles to the forearm

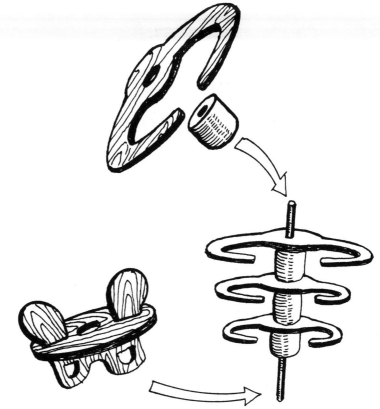

Fig. 6-2. Ribs and pelvis of the skeleton.

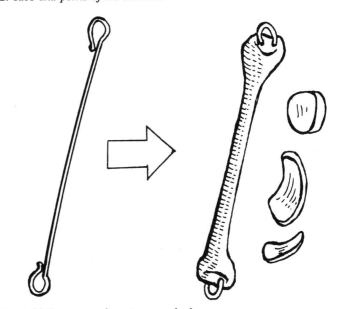

Fig. 6-3. Mold Fimo around a wire to make bones.

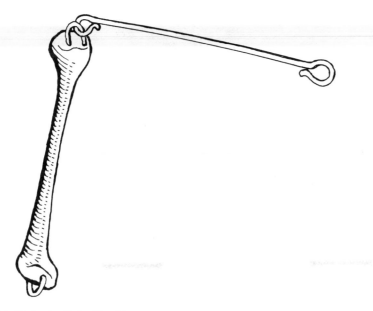

Fig. 6-4. Make the limbs like this.

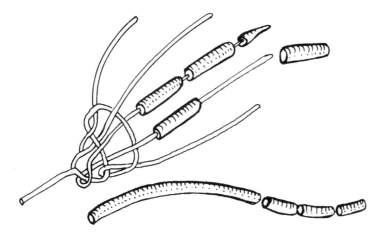

Fig. 6-5. Make hands by attaching Fimo to wire.

and lower leg *before* adding the Fimo. Fingers and toes can be made by rolling narrow tubes of Fimo, cutting them into sections, then stringing the sections on the wires like beads (FIG. 6-5). Ribs, shoulders, and pelvis are made in the same way. These are all joined together to make one solid torso (FIG. 6-6).

The skeleton is strung up in such a way that the puppeteer has only to tilt the vertical wooden control to cause the puppet's arms and legs to fall off. Holding the control upright restores the limbs. Study FIG. 6-7 to see how this is done.

Note that the arms are not jointed to the shoulders but dangle on two strings (FIG. 6-7E), which pass through holes in the shoulder. The thigh strings (D) pass

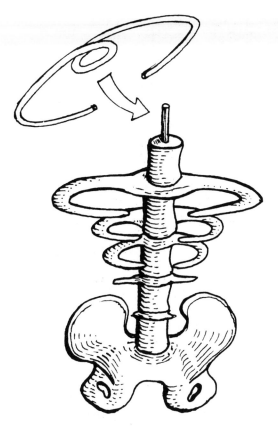

Fig. 6-6. Ribs, shoulders, and pelvis are made of Fimo and joined together.

through the same two holes in the shoulder, and they pass through two holes in the hips as well. Both strings run from the puppet to the upper bar of the control. When the control is tilted forward the upper bar goes down, and the limbs also go down. The puppet is equipped with a pair of normal hand strings (G) and knee strings (F). These allow you to control the skeleton exactly as you would a normal puppet, when the control is in the vertical position. When the control is tilted, you can use the hand and leg strings to control the puppet's detached limbs, drawing them further away from the skeleton's rib cage and pelvis.

Two strings (C) run from the skeleton's shoulders to a crossbar on the lower end of the control. These serve a dual purpose. In the first place, they support the puppet's full weight. When the crutch is tilted, the bottom end of the control moves up and the puppet's torso rises as well. These two strings also serve to guide the head when it is lifted from the puppet's shoulders.

A single string (B) runs from a screw eye on the skeleton's clavicle straight through a hole in the head to a screw eye mounted on the lower end of the crossbar. Finally, a string (A) runs from the top of the puppet's head, through a screw eye on the centerpiece of the crutch to a ring. When the puppeteer pulls on this ring the head rises. When the ring is released the head drops back into place.

119

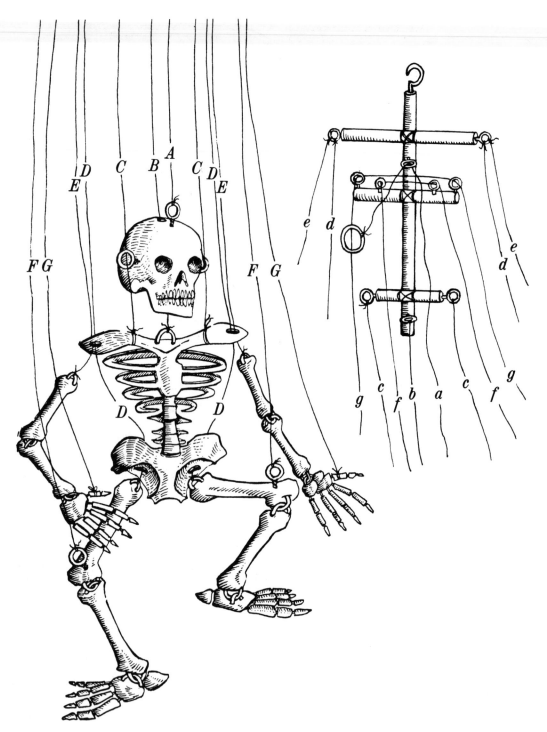

Fig. 6-7. Stringing the disjointing skeleton.

THE WEIGHTLIFTER

This weightlifter is quite simple, compared to the disjointing skeleton, but he is far more interesting to watch than you might think (FIG. 6-8). He not only lifts his barbells, but he balances them on his head and feet.

When the curtain comes up, the barbell is on the floor and the puppet is standing over it. He bows modestly, first to one side of the auditorium, then to the other. Then he sets to work. He bends over the barbell and places his two hands under it. He adjusts his stance, and begins straining at the weights, but they don't budge. He throws himself into it again, groaning pitiably. This time the barbell rises an inch or so off the stage floor, before falling back (a backstage confederate can add to the realism by making a loud clang or thud at precisely the right moment). A drum roll starts as he tries one last time, his whole body shuddering with the effort. In a clash of cymbals the puppet stands up straight, hoisting the barbell over his head. Then he lowers the bar onto his head and drops his hands to his side. He sways back and forth, struggling to keep his balance while the 2000-pound weight teeters precariously. The weight drops to the ground, and he takes another bow.

You will notice that the illustration does not show all the strings necessary to work a normal puppet. To reduce confusion in the illustration, I left out some of the strings that are found on an ordinary marionette (back of the head, knees, etc.) The two strings that are attached to the toes of the weightlifter's slippers serve only to guide the barbell as it rises and falls. The two hand strings (FIG. 6-8A) run from a detachable crosspiece, through the barbell, to the palm of the puppet's hands. These strings must be long enough to allow the barbell to rest on the floor while the puppet is standing up straight (FIG. 6-9).

Pulling up on the detachable crosspiece brings the barbell directly to the puppet's hands. Pulling the bar higher raises the hands and barbell together. There are two other strings (FIG. 6-9C) attached to the ends of the weight. These run to a second detachable crossbar. By raising or lowering this bar you can control the movement of the barbell without affecting the hands.

THE SPLIT GOLIATH

Goliath shuffles on stage, looking big and hairy and scary. He's swinging a twisted wooden club, looking around for someone to pulverize with it. David creeps up behind. Instead of running in terror from the giant warrior (a 19 incher, at the very least), David aims his sling and calls his enemy's name. Goliath wheels about, and in that same instant David launches a rock at his forehead. The giant reels, staggers, and, to the audience's combined revulsion and delight, splits into two parts. With a triumphant shout, David disperses the halves of Goliath's body. The two halves hop off in opposite directions, and the scene ends (FIG. 6-10).

Goliath is a fairly ordinary puppet, except that he happens to be sliced down the middle. In fact, you should build the body as a single puppet and then saw it in two with a fine-bladed saw after it is complete. Note that the hips and torso are a single piece of wood. Otherwise, Goliath is made in the usual way. Like the body, the head is split into two halves. It doesn't matter whether the head

Fig. 6-8. The weightlifter.

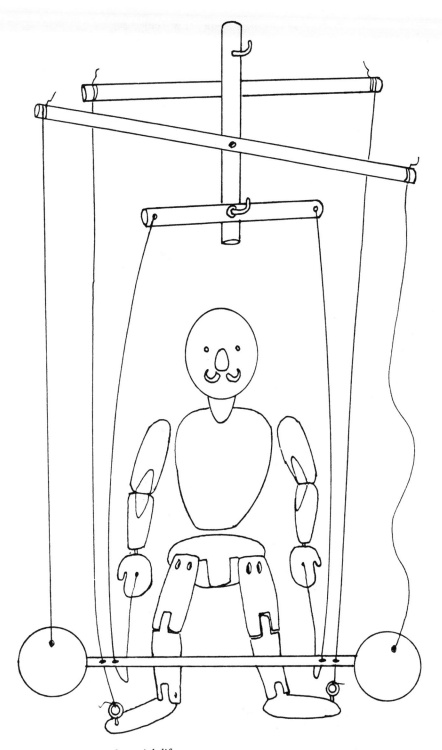

Fig. 6-9. Stringing the weightlifter.

is hollow or solid, but don't attempt to model or sculpt the halves separately. Make a single head and then slice it in two. To disguise the seam, give Goliath bushy whiskers and a good head of hair as well. Each half of the neck has its own screw eye, for obvious reasons.

Strings A, B and C on FIG. 6-10 run through holes in one side of Goliath's head and torso, and are firmly anchored on the inside of the other half of the body. When the strings are pulled tight, the puppet is held together; but when they are permitted to fall slack, there is nothing to keep Goliath from falling in two. The marionette control is also in two halves (FIG. 6-11).

The two halves of the control are held together with long strips of Velcro, or elastic ribbon, if you prefer. The parts of the control are made with comparatively thick slats of wood so that they are easy to fasten securely together. When the puppeteer wishes to divide the marionette, he releases strings A, B and C (FIG. 6-10), and permits them to fall to the stage floor. Then he unfastens the Velcro, separates the two parts of the control, and hands one of the parts to another puppeteer. As the two sections of Goliath's body run off in opposite directions, the strings A, B, and C pass without impediment through the holes in his head and torso.

The seam in Goliath's body can be concealed with rumpled clothing, a shaggy cape, or some sort of distinctive armored breastplate. The audience will not be expecting to see the puppet fall in two, so it is unlikely that they'll notice the seam. People tend to see only what they expect to see, as any stage conjuror knows.

THE THREE-HEADED SCARAMOUCHE

''Scaramouche'' comes from the Italian *commedia dell'arte,* a style of masked comic theatre that flourished between the sixteenth and the eighteenth centuries. The *commedia* was carried throughout Europe by troupes of Italian actors. In order to make themselves understood in the different countries to which they traveled, the *commedia* showmen developed a style of improvisational comedy that used few words and relied heavily on stock characters. Some of these characters are still widely known: Harlequin, Pierrot and, of course, the immortal Pulcinello, better known these days as Punch.

Although the true *commedia* is long gone, most of the stock characters have gone on to other things. Pierrot, for instance, has become enormously popular as a porcelain-headed doll, and Harlequin is widely associated with paperback romance novels. Punch made it big as a hand puppet (after a brief stint as a well-bred marionette in the puppet parlours of eighteenth century London). But the stock character Scaramuccia, a boastful coward, has been almost entirely forgotten.

Like Punch, Scaramuccia, or Scaramouche, as the puppet version is known, went into puppetry after the death of the *commedia* theatre. However he seems to have degenerated into a novelty act quite soon after he entered the business. By the early nineteenth century the word Scaramouche is used to refer to any grotesque and outlandish specialty puppet. The Scaramouche often had a minor role in the puppet shows that starred Mr. Punch. He would come on briefly to

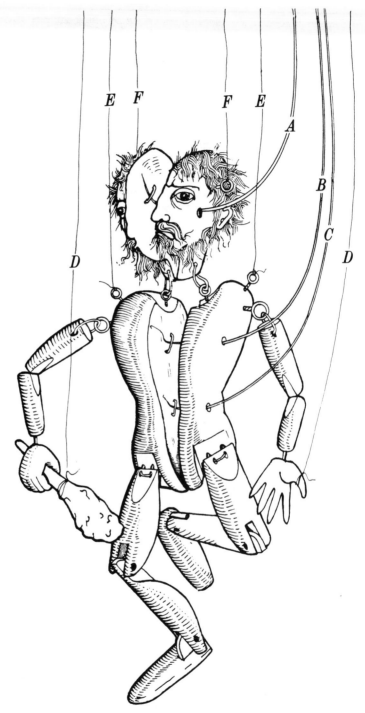

Fig. 6-10. The split Goliath.

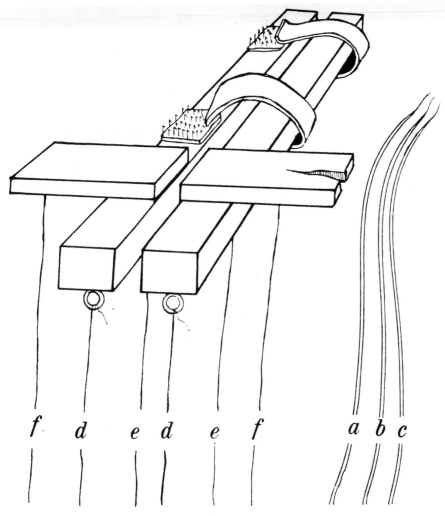

Fig. 6-11. The control for the Goliath is also in two parts.

perform some bizarre trick, after which he was clubbed to death, like everyone who shared a stage with Punch.

On the marionette stage, the Scaramouche's tricks usually seem to have involved his head and neck. He might run on stage as a headless body and then transform himself into a bodiless head. Or else his neck might suddenly become tremendously long and flexible. Nasty as these tricks must have been, none could have rivaled the freakish absurdity of the three-headed Scaramouche.

The three-headed Scaramouche begins his routine with no head at all. The body runs in from the wings, gesticulating wildly. He has lost his head. A puppet Samaritan appears on the scene. Seeing the Scaramouche's predicament, he advises the poor creature to give up on finding his old head and concentrate on growing a new one. To speed the process along, the Samaritan sprinkles various fertilizers

Fig. 6-12. The three-headed Scaramouche.

over the bare shoulders: plant food, multivitamins, hair tonic, and a spoonful of yeast. Then he leads the Scaramouche to a mirror while the latter sprouts first one head, then another, then one more on top of those. The Scramouche chases his helper off the stage (FIG. 6-12).

This is one of the easier trick puppets to make. The three heads are hollow and are designed to nest inside one another like salad bowls. Make them as you would any papier-mâché head, leaving a round hole big enough for the smaller heads to pass though. Put a fringe of decorative ribbon or lace around the holes. A tube of cloth forms a neck, which connects the bottom of the smaller head to the rim of the hole in the larger head. Use glue to attach the neck tube to the rim (FIG. 6-13).

Fig. 6-13. The hollow body of the Scaramouche.

The hollow body can be made of a tin can, covered with papier-mâché. The tin can is attached to the arms and pelvis in the same way as an ordinary wooden torso. The can must be roomy enough to contain the largest head. If the hands and feet are fairly small in relation to the Scaramouche's stout body, he will look particularly grotesque. Each of the heads has two strings, so that it may be lifted and moved independently.

THE EXTENDABLE MAN

The extendable man transforms himself from a dwarf to a giant in full view of the audience. He can also shrink from giant to dwarf, and can go on fluctuating in this way until the trick is no longer funny. This puppet takes the principle of the traditional neck-stretching Scaramouche and extends it (so to to speak) to the whole body. It is essentially a novelty puppet, but it is not hard to imagine using the technique in a narrative show. There are plenty of familiar stories in which small people are supposed to grow magically large. In a puppet version of Alice in Wonderland, this might provide a way of staging the scene where her neck grows (FIG. 6-14).

The extendable man has no body of the conventional sort. He is made of wooden disks connected by lengths of ribbon or string. The leg disks can be sliced like baloney from a thick piece of dowelling. The disks of the upper body should be made of thin plywood, while the shoulder segment may be carved from a scrap of softwood (choose a piece whose grain runs horizontally). The head, arms, and hands are made in the usual way. The pieces are connected together with strands of ribbon or supple cord. These must bend easily so that the puppet collapses properly. The same goes for this marionette's clothing. Dress the extendable man in a fine knit cloth. Thick, woven cloth will not fold well when he collapses.

AN ANIMAL

This is not, properly speaking, a stunt puppet. However, this seemed like the best place to include an example of a four-footed marionette.

The donkey's body shown in FIG. 6-15 is made of a solid piece of wood. The legs are hinged against the sides of the wooden body. The flanks must be quite flat to allow the legs to swivel without hindrance. You might find it most convenient to cut the body shape out of plywood, rounding it out with foam and fabric later on. Glue two pieces of thick plywood together and cut the shape with a jigsaw. This provides a basic flat-sided form that can be refined later.

The donkey has a segmented neck, a feature which gives his head complete freedom of movement. The segments are cut from a single solid neck carved into a donkeyesque shape. The segments are drilled through and strung together like beads on a sturdy cord. You can hide the segments with a layer of stretchy cloth or fake fur, but you might find that they actually add to the strange appeal of the animal. The head should be made of papier-mâché.

THE GRAND TURK

The Grand Turk was invented sometime during the first half of the nineteenth century. He seems to have been an instant sensation: by Queen Victoria's time

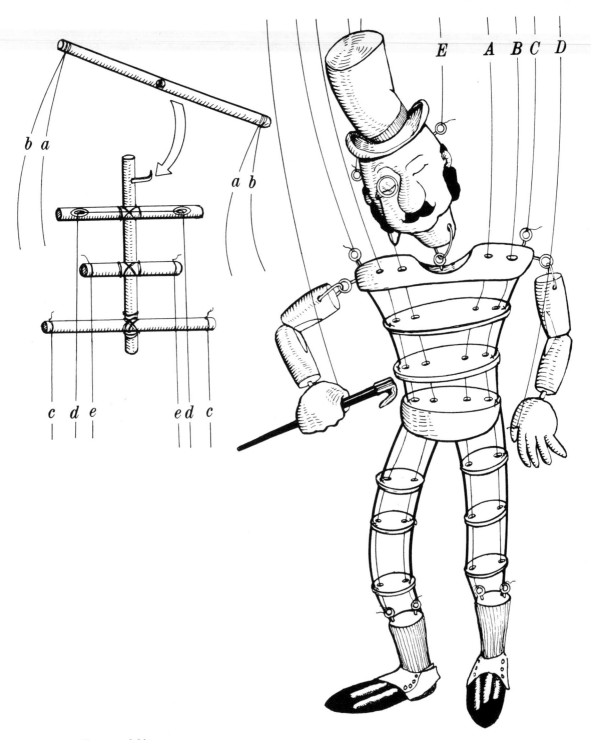

Fig. 6-14. The extendable man.

Fig. 6-15. A donkey.

virtually every marionette troupe had a Grand Turk in the company. His trick is even more outlandish than that of the three-headed Scaramouche. The Grand Turk swaggers in, resplendently dressed and very full of himself. As it turns out, he is not only full of himself—he is full of six other puppets. With sufficient provocation, the Grand Turk will transform himself into six lesser Turks.

Obviously, this is not the sort of puppet that you can use in every show. However, because he's a proven crowd pleaser, you might want to create a pretext for including him. He could be useful on any scene that involves combat.

131

For instance, a cowardly sorceror in a tight spot might conjure up the Grand Turk to be his magical champion. When the Turk is attacked, he splits apart into six manic dwarves who mob the opponent (FIG. 6-16).

You might wonder why this transformation puppet is a Grand Turk and not a Grand Bus Conductor or a Grand Mailman. The reason has to do with the mechanics of his stunt. The puppet has five puppets hidden inside his body, so it is essential that the marionette be dressed in baggy clothing that fits tightly around the wrists and ankles. The huge turban provides a convenient place to hide a sixth puppet, and because the turban need not have any shape or structure, it is quite easy to make entirely out of cloth. Offhand, I can think of only one other kind of hat that would be sufficiently voluminous to contain a whole puppet: the traditional cook's hat. I suppose it would be possible to create a Grand Chef puppet who would split apart into six tiny pastry cooks. But the apron and open cuffs of the cooks' costume would interfere with the mechanism that hides the other puppets.

As you can see from FIG. 6-16, the Grand Turk has no body; he is made of his own clothing. Every limb has a miniature puppet head inside it, attached at the neck to the inside of the cuff. Each of the Turk's arms and legs is composed of a baggy tube of fabric which, when turned inside out, serves as a caftan for a tiny puppet. The turban and torso contain two more inside-out miniatures. FIGURE 6-17 shows how they are concealed.

Notice that there are two nails protruding through the shoulders of the puppet (the cloth is slit to accommodate them). These will provide hooks to hold the rings by which the arms and legs are attached. The rings are stacked onto these hooks. Each limb-puppet has a string running from its head, around the stack of rings, and up to a crossbar on the control. This string passes under the lowest ring on the stack, so that when it is pulled the rings are lifted off the nail and the limb comes free. The cloth then falls, revealing the head and arms of the concealed puppet. It might be necessary to weight the cloth so that it falls correctly.

When the arms and legs have all been detached, the torso and turban undergo a similar transformation. The strings that gather the rings together (FIG. 6-17A) are released and allowed to fall loose to the stage below. Gravity pulls the weighted cloth of the turban down to reveal the puppet inside. The Grand Turk is no more.

The control is nothing more than a bar with hooks for the rings which are attached to the heads of the various lesser Turks. The ring-gathering string is anchored in a slot on one end of the control ready to be released quickly (FIG. 6-18).

The Grand Turk has no hand, head, and feet strings, and consequently does not move very well. You can add such strings, but they will have to be released and allowed to fall loosely to the stage *before* the puppet is dismantled, or else they will prevent the cloth tubes of the limbs and turban from turning themselves inside out. Even with such strings added, the Grand Turk is not likely to move in a very orderly or elegant manner. Don't allow much time to elapse between his initial entrance and his disintegration stunt.

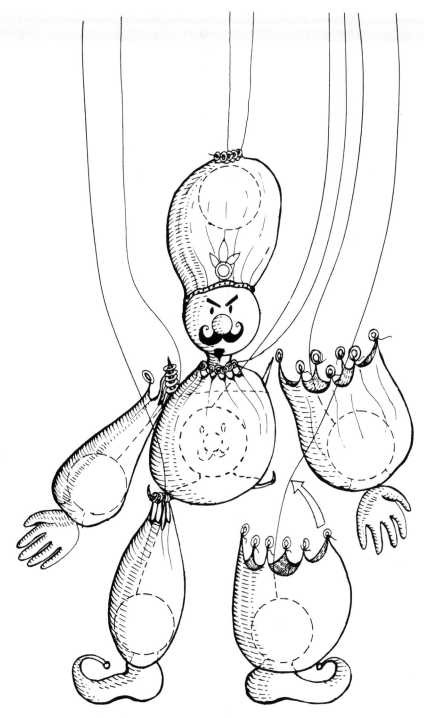

Fig. 6-16. *The Grand Turk.*

Fig. 6-17. Miniature puppets disguised inside the Grand Turk.

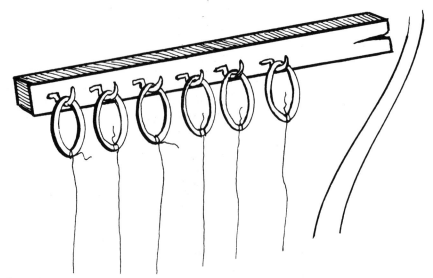

Fig. 6-18. The control for the Grand Turk.

VII

Stage, Stage Lights, and Play

A booth diminutive there stood
Where pygmy actors made of wood
Were leaning o'er a canvas clout
And squeaking to the rabble rout.

"Hudibras Redivivus," (1705)

Ned Ward,

IN THE BODLEIAN LIBRARY AT OXFORD UNIVERSITY THERE IS A DELIGHTFULLY illustrated manuscript dating from 1344. It tells a rather interesting version of the story of Alexander the Great, but that isn't why I mention it. In the margin of one of the pages there is a painted miniature showing two hand puppets. It is the oldest known portrayal of a European puppet play. In this little drawing, the puppets are behaving exactly as glove puppets do today: one is threatening the other with a large stick. The illumination is particularly valuable because it gives us a good look at a fourteenth century puppet stage. It shows that a curtain was used to hide the puppeteers. It shows a kind of arch stretching over the puppet's heads, seemingly to mark out their performing space. And it shows two miniature castle towers rising on each side of the stage. Apparently, the puppet stage was set up to look like a medieval fortress, as if the play were being enacted on the battlements, while the audience looked on from below. To this day the French word for "puppet stage" is *castellet*—"little castle."

No doubt many of the plays that were acted out on the walls of this "little castle" told of chivalry and battles, as the Sicilian marionettes do to this day. Quite likely there was no more scenery onstage than the two towers, which also served to support the curtain behind which the puppeteers concealed themselves. With so little scenery, the stage could be dismantled quickly and reassembled somewhere else, for in those days puppeteers lived like nomads, carrying their equipment from one small village to the next.

When Italian-style string marionettes became widely popular in the seventeenth century, the puppet stage became a more elaborate affair. By this time puppeteers had begun to play in permanent or semipermanent theatres, which made it possible to mount extremely sophisticated productions in which the stage not only concealed the manipulators but supported a series of richly detailed scenes. The stage was no longer a "little castle" but a "little world." Puppeteers began to rely on special effects requiring ingenious mechanisms to convince the audience that this world was real. Thus, the marionette theatre as we know it today came into being.

The puppeteer's lot hasn't changed much. It is still extremely difficult for puppeteers to stay put, and it is a very fortunate marionette company that can afford to install itself in a permanent theatre. To make a living, most companies must travel, and so simple economics ensures that the long tradition of the itinerant puppet troupe will continue.

Every company has different needs. Some are large and established, and can stay in one place. some own or rent large trucks to carry tons of equipment from one venue to the next. Most, however, must compromise. They must be able to fit an entire production into a fairly small vehicle without skimping on props, special effects, scenery, or any of the things that make a marionette show memorable. Later in this chapter I'll provide plans for a complete marionette stage that can be moved from place to place. First, however, we will take a look at some of the alternatives that are available to those who wish to mount a performance but would like to spare themselves the work of staging a full-blown, classical string puppet show.

A SIMPLE STAGE

The simplest kind of stage is no stage at all. A marionette show can be performed with the puppeteers in full view of the audience. In the traditional Japanese *Bunraku* puppet theatre, each character is operated by three different manipulators, none of them hidden from the spectators. The puppeteers—as many as 30 or 40 of them in a typical performance—dress in black costumes, with their faces concealed under black hoods. Black clothing helps the audience to ignore the puppeteers, but it is by no means necessary. If the manipulators are efficient and skillful, the audience will succeed in ignoring them, no matter how they are dressed. It all depends on how you set up the audience's expectations. If you make it clear immediately that you are not attempting to hide yourself, then the audience will very quickly forget you are there. On the other hand, if you decide to conceal yourself behind a curtain or backdrop you had better do a good job of it, because once the audience expects you to remain out of sight they will certainly be distracted if you come into view by mistake.

The important thing is to give the audience what they've come to see—or more. If the spectators at a horror movie can easily tell that King Kong is just some guy in a gorilla suit, they will feel cheated. But take the same audience to the shoddiest puppet show, featuring three ham actors in street clothes jiggling a papier-mâché dragon, and they will enthusiastically applaud. Why? Because the performers are obeying the first principle of good showmanship: always give the audience more than they bargained for, and *don't* promise anything you can't deliver. If you tell the crowd that the hand is quicker than the eye, it had better be.

Some of the most elegant and moving puppet plays are performed without elaborate scenery and "stage magic." In fact, it is probably easier to play upon the crowd's emotions when you are not simultaneously struggling to maintain an illusion. Merely keeping the manipulators hidden is a surprisingly big job, requiring a fairly elaborate system of backdrops, side panels, curtains and controlled lighting. All of these can get in the way of the puppets and restrict their mobility, particularly in a string puppet show, and this will tend to dissipate the emotional tension and energy of the play. On an elevated marionette stage the puppeteers generally don't have a lot of elbow room. Something as simple as making one puppet cross in front of the other requires one manipulator to duck under another puppeteer's arms. Eliminating the hazards of a confined stage frees the performers to concentrate on subtleties of movement and dramatic expression.

If you are thinking of putting on a puppet play but don't want to tackle a full production, then by all means consider doing one without a true stage. A section of your room or hall can be marked off as the performing space and you can operate the puppets right on the floor. Schools, churches, and community centers often have wooden risers, or even full stages with lighting equipment already installed. You might be able to make good use of these.

When the puppeteers are in full view of the audience, it is best if they do not speak the puppets' lines. The sight of the manipulator talking a character's part as he works the strings will distract the audience. It is much better to have narrator or narrators standing apart, reciting the action of the story and performing the puppets' voice. This is the way Japanese Bunraku theatre is done, and it is very effective.

Position the narrators at either side of the stage area. When the narrator speaks a part, move a puppet's head and hands as if he or she is doing the talking. One person can perform several roles while simultaneously narrating the events of the story. There's usually no need to conceal the narrator; in fact you might wish to incorporate him or her into the action of the play (FIG. 7-1).

A MORE ADVANCED STAGE

Even if you decide to perform with the puppeteers in full view, you might wish to have scenery in the background behind the puppets. There's no reason why this should pose a problem; all you need is something to support the scenery while the puppeteers go about their business. There are several simple ways to do this, depending on what kind of scenery you need, where you're going to perform, and how much work you want to put into building the stage apparatus. Assuming

Fig. 7-1. The puppeteer need not be concealed.

the scenic backdrops are made of cloth, you can simply drape them over a horizontal bar raised to a suitable height. The bar can be made out of anything that is sufficiently long and strong enough to support your backdrops. A wooden 2 × 2 should be about right, or a long piece of heavy dowelling. You could also use a metal pole such as an extendable closet rack or curtain rod. However, you'll probably find it easier to nail your cloth scenes to wood than to try to fasten them to a metal bar.

Lash the two ends of the pole to two high-backed chairs (or coat racks, lampstands, etc.) as in FIG. 7-2. This elementary stage allows you to make swift, graceful scene changes. Sew or glue the top edges of the different scenes together like the pages of book. Fasten the ''spine'' of the book to the horizontal bar and flip the scenes over as you need them. Don't attempt to hide the scene change from the audience (you won't be able to anyway). If it is done efficiently and with a flourish, it will probably contribute to their enjoyment of the show.

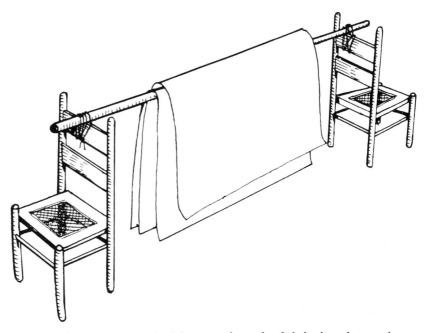

Fig. 7-2. For a simple stage, backdrops can be made of cloth, draped over a bar.

There is one drawback to this backdrop. Because it hangs like a curtain, the scenery tends to move around. Every room has its draughts, and you will certainly create air currents as you move behind the scene. Your audience might be disturbed at the sight of the Rocky Mountains or the Great Pyramids of Giza wafting gently in front of the air conditioner. You can minimize this by painting your scenery on very heavy cloth, or by attaching weights to the lower edge of the backdrop. Shops that carry sewing supplies often sell lead curtain weights for just this purpose. You might also try attaching loops of elastic ribbon (also available at sewing shops) to the bottom hem of the backdrop and fastening these around hooks mounted on the floor.

Finally, you might decide to mount each scene on a separate rigid frame. This kind of backdrop is known in the theatre world as a ''flat''. Build a wooden stretcher with slats of 1- ×-2-inch softwood. Use metal angle brackets (available at any hardware store) on the insides of the four corners to make the stretcher perfectly rectangular (FIG. 7-3). Stretch the scenery over the wooden frame, attaching the cloth with wood staples or carpet tacks. To stretch the cloth as tightly

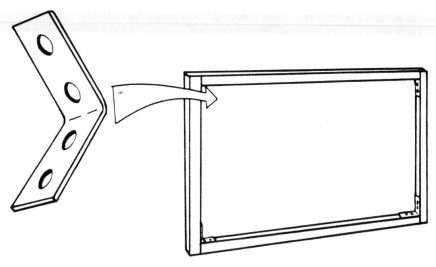

Fig. 7-3. For a more advanced stage, flats can be used for scenery.

as possible, you should begin in the middle of each wooden slat and work your way out toward the four corners.

If you are using flats, there's no longer any need to hang the scenes from above. Simply rest them on the floor and lean them against the horizontal bar. It's a good idea to place two blocks on the floor in front of the lower edge to keep the bottoms of the scenes from slipping forward (FIG. 7-4).

The different backdrops can be stacked somewhere behind the stage until they are needed. Scene changes will involve removing one flat and installing another. Keep the audience distracted while you go about your business. Sing, tell jokes, comment on the story. Play the flute with one hand while you move scenes with the other. The audience will admire your audacity as much as your skill. With experience you will find that there are many ways to incorporate scene changes into the show.

A FULL MARIONETTE STAGE

The most celebrated of all string marionettes, Pinocchio, knew he was only a puppet and wanted to be a real boy. In my opinion that is the secret ambition of every string marionette: to pass for human. On a true marionette stage, with full scenery and controlled lighting, that ambition is very nearly realized. Young children are fully prepared to believe that the marionettes are living, breathing beings. And the child within every adult continues to delight in being fooled, long after he or she is old enough to know better.

On the other hand, although most of us love to be cleverly deceived, we are always on guard against it. Illusions are fragile, and the illusionist must conceal all evidence of his subterfuge. The main problem, as you can imagine, is the very elementary one of hiding the puppeteers from the audience. The manipulators must be able to control all that happens on the stage without actually appearing

Fig. 7-4. Rest the flats on the floor, against a bar, and use blocks to keep them from slipping.

upon it. This requires that scenery and stage curtains be carefully positioned so as to give the spectators an unobstructed view of everything except the puppeteers.

To give those in the back rows a clear view of the action, it is necessary to raise the puppets a couple of feet off the ground. In a Punch-and-Judy-type show, this is easy. In fact, it is unavoidable, because the actors must stand or crouch below the stage "floor," holding the puppets over their heads (FIG. 7-5). A marionette show is a different matter. If the puppets must be raised, the puppeteers must be raised still higher, which necessitates a fairly sturdy stage, capable of bearing the full weight of three or four manipulators in the throes of performance.

For a marionette show, the panel or curtain that hides the puppeteers must be about as high as the tops of their heads. So, if the puppeteers are standing 2 feet above ground level, the stage must be about 8 feet high. As you can see, we are talking about a rather large and elaborate structure. Then there's the width of the stage to think about. The stage floor that the marionettes walk around on will be about 3 or 4 feet wide, but the entire stage must be considerably wider.

Fig. 7-5. A back view of a Victorian hand-puppet stage. Etching by George Cruikshank (1873).

The audience will not be sitting in a straight line in front of the stage. They will fan out from the front of your stage so that those on the sides near the back of the room might be in a terrible position to see the marionettes, but ideally situated for seeing the puppeteers moving around behind the stage. To prevent this, your stage, or at least the curtain which hides the puppeteers, must be 14 to 16 feet wide.

By now you might be thinking you've let yourself in for a major construction project. Well, it's not really that bad. I'm stressing the problems of designing a stage so that we can get a clear picture of them and, I hope, avoid unplanned problems. If you are alert to the difficulty of creating clear sight lines, then you will be able to build a stage that provides adequate viewing conditions for your entire audience.

In the following pages I will provide designs for an easy-to build and portable stage that can be adapted to the needs of most troupes. Anybody with a drill and a saw can build this stage, and anybody with a little ingenuity can probably improve on it. This design is not meant to be ideal for all purposes, in fact, it is lacking features that many professional marionette troupes feel are essential. For instance, in most professional companies the platform that the puppeteers stand on (the ''bridge'' as it is called) is about a foot higher than the floor the puppets walk on. The puppeteers rest their arms and upper bodies on a ''leaning bar,'' which makes performing more comfortable (FIG. 7-6).

In the design that follows, I have eliminated the bridge and leaning bar. The puppeteers will stand on the same level as the puppets. The reason for this is

Fig. 7-6. Performing is more comfortable with a leaning bar.

very simple: The leaning bar and raised platform make scene changes more difficult.

Without the leaning bar blocking the way, it is possible to remove the floor the puppets stand on and replace it with another. You can attach scenery and props directly to the various stage floors, which allows you to include some very elaborate installations onstage without having to worry about setting them up and taking them down between scenes. When it comes time to change the scene, you simply remove one floor and insert another. Even a speedy scene change can seem interminable, so you might be grateful for any seconds you can shave off. After trying this stage you might find you can't live without a leaning bar and raised bridge. In that case, you have only to add one. This design is quite flexible and easily modified.

Apart from quick scene changes, the chief virtue of this design is that you will not need a convoy of flat-bed trucks to transport it from place to place. It should fit quite neatly into a van, pickup truck, or trailer. Unfortunately, you won't be able to take it on the subway. Like I said, I've made compromises. Note: Before starting work, read the following instructions carefully and study the diagrams.

Materials

- Wood in the following lengths (If possible, have the plywood pre-cut at the lumber yard to save trouble. Buy 8-foot long spruce 2 × 6s and 2 × 4s—the straightest you can find):
    (2) 2 × 6s, 8 feet long.
    (4) 2 × 4s, 8 feet long.
    (2) sheets of ½ inch plywood, 6 × 2 ½ feet.
    (2) sheets of ½ inch plywood, 1 foot wide and 2 ¾ feet long.
    (1) sheet of ¾- or 1-inch plywood, 6 × 2 ½ feet.

- Carriage bolts, wing nuts, and washers, in the following sizes:
    (14) bolts, 3 ½ inches long.
    (4) bolts, 7 inches long.
    (12) bolts 4 ¼ inches long.

- Two L-shaped metal bars. (If these are not available, use wood.)
- Nine yards of opaque black cloth, 60 inches wide. (You don't have to spend a lot of money on this material, but you must select it carefully. When you hold it up to a lamp or window you should be unable to see specks of light through it.)
- Strips of Velcro (to attach the curtain).

---

1. Start with two 2 × 6s (a1 and a2 in FIG. 7-7). Cut these to a length of 5 ½ feet. Use the leftover stock to make the two short back supports, (b1 and b2). These back supports should be 2 ½ feet in length.

2. The two tall curtain supports, (c1 and c2) are made of 2 × 4s, as are the bottom braces, (d1 and d2). The curtain supports are a full 8 feet long. Cut each bottom brace to a length of 5 ½ feet.

3. All the separate elements of this stage are joined together with carriage bolts and wing nuts (available at any hardware store). This allows you to dismantle the apparatus easily. Use bolts about 3 ½ inches long and at least ⅜ inches in diameter. You will need 14 bolts for the two sides of the stage shown in FIG. 7-7. Drill holes for the bolts and assemble as in the illustration.

4. You will need three sheets of plywood (FIG. 7-8). Sheet A in the illustration must be as sturdy a piece as you can find, because it will support the weight of the puppeteers. Plywood 1 inch thick is ideal. If necessary, ¾ inch

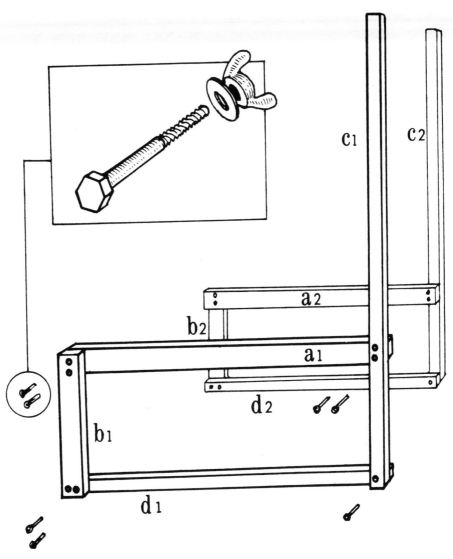

Fig. 7-7. The frame of the marionette stage.

will suffice. Pre-cut sheet A to a size of 6 × 2 ½ feet. Attach to the top of the stage (a1 and a2 in FIG. 7-7), using four carriage bolts, each 7 inches long.

5. Sheets B and C (FIG. 7-8) should be cut from lighter plywood: ⅜ or ½ inch will do. The sheets should be pre-cut to a size of 6 × 2 ½ feet. Fasten them to the top and bottom of the two long curtain supports with 4-inch carriage bolts. Finally, add on the two side panels (D1 an D2), each cut to a size of 1 × 3 feet. This will create a "window" (3 feet high and 4 feet wide), through which the audience will watch the puppets.

6. Attach the two horizontal curtain rods (FIG. 7-9). To support the curtain, use two L-shaped metal bars, such as are used for scaffolding or heavy metal

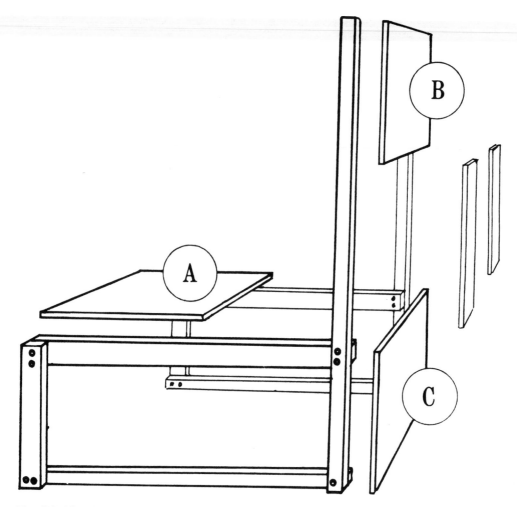

Fig. 7-8. The plywood must be sturdy to support the puppeteers.

shelves. If these bars are not available, substitute some other type of metal bar, or even or pair of wooden 2 × 2 s. Remember that the horizontal bars must be strong enough to support a large quantity of fairly heavy cloth. Each bar should be about 8 feet long so that the curtains project 5 feet out from each side of the stage opening.

7. To make the curtain you will need about 8 yards of opaque black cloth. Cut the cloth into four pieces, and attach them to the front of the stage with strips of Velcro. Use epoxy or contact cement to attach the Velcro to the wood and/or metal of the stage.

8. The main structure of the stage is finished. The floors that the puppets stand on can be made out of sheets of plywood ⅜ inch thick. You will need as many different floors as there are different scenes in your play. Each floor sits flat on the same 2 × 6s that support the puppeteer's bridge, where it may be

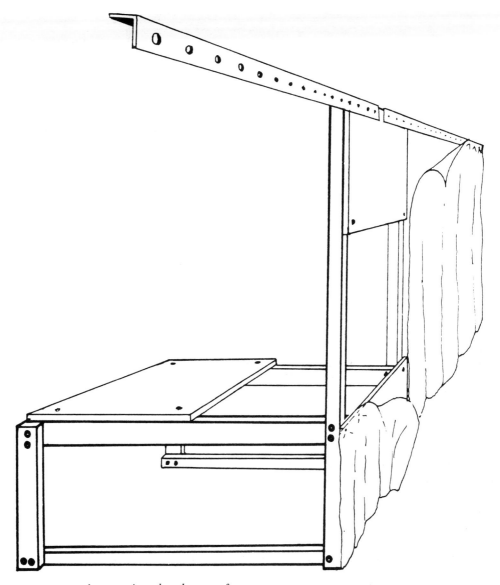

Fig. 7-9. Attach a curtain rod to the stage frame.

easily removed and replaced. The stage lights and stage curtain are mounted on the upper plywood sheet (FIG. 7-8). The puppeteers manipulate the marionettes from behind, leaning over the stretched cloth backdrop (FIG. 7-10).

You will notice in the above illustration that the backdrop is considerably wider and taller than the stage opening itself. This is to prevent the audience from seeing past the edges of the scenery. (Even so, you will have to make sure the spectators do not sit too close to the stage: the closer they sit, the wider their viewing angle will be). The backdrops should be theatrical flats, (which were

Fig. 7-10. A puppeteer using the stage.

were described in this chapter under "A More Advanced Stage"). Make them about 4 feet high and 6 feet wide. Each backdrop is pegged to the 2 × 6s that run from the front to the back of the stage (FIG. 7-11 a and b) with pieces of ¾ inch dowelling. This system allows you to remove and replace the backdrops easily. Fix the dowelling pegs permanently in the bottom slats of the wooden stretchers (FIG. 7-12).

Drill a hole in each of the 2 × 6s so that the backdrop dowels fit snugly but can be removed without difficulty. (To drill holes up to ¾ inch in diameter you will need a special "auger" bit. These can be fitted to any electric drill with a ¼-inch chuck.)

Note: The peg-and-hole system described above for backdrops is equally useful for attaching objects and scenery to the stage floors themselves. In particular,

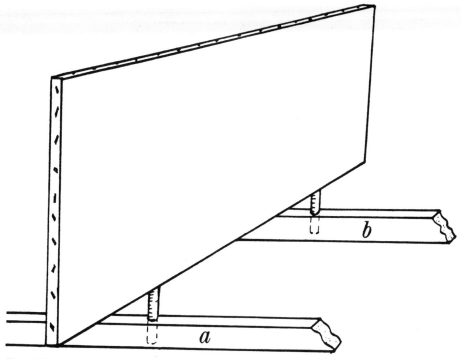

Fig. 7-11. The backdrops are pegged into place for easy removal.

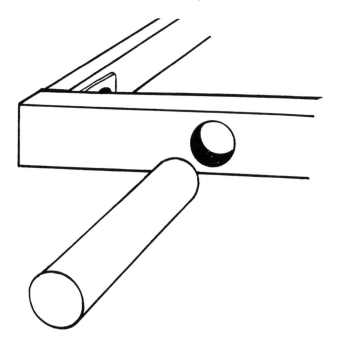

Fig. 7-12. The dowelling pegs.

149

Fig. 7-13. The pegging system is also used for attaching objects to the stage floor.

every scene should have "wings" at either end of the stage opening to prevent the audience from seeing out the sides. These can be pegged right to the floors (FIG. 7-13). Wings perform two functions. They block the audience's view out the sides of the stage opening, and they provide support for foreground scenery, which can add depth to a setting.

LIGHTING

I'm sure I don't need to point out the advantages of adequate stage lighting. Without it your show will be invisible. At the very least, you must supply enough light to make all the important features of the show stand out clearly. The smaller the puppets, the more of a problem this will be.

Of course, lighting, when it is used well, does more than merely show off the details of scenery and expression. Stage lighting is one of the most effective ways to create atmosphere. Appropriate lighting casts the mood of the entire scene.

It can add dramatic dimension to the most ordinary scenery. In some cases lighting can even allow you to dispense with scenery altogether.

Suppose you are making a tropical storm. Instead of painting thunderclouds directly on the cloth backdrop, you can have the storm appear gradually by building it entirely with light. Illuminate a plain grey cloth from behind to make a sky backlit with streaks of red and troubled by flashes of lightning. To suggest a torchlit grotto you could throw a fiery, orange glow over the entire scene, lighting the puppets from below so that they cast eerie shadows on the cavern walls. You might even invent a mechanism to make the light seem to flicker and pulse. These are only a few of the effects you can get with lighting. In the Chapter VIII we will look at other lighting tricks. For the present we'll concentrate on creating a simple wash of white light that will allow most of the audience to see most of the action in the play.

A minimal lighting system must be able to bathe the whole stage opening in white light, so that the audience can distinguish all the important details of character and scenery. Even if you are performing without a full stage, you must light the performing area. In fact, if you are performing without scenery, lighting will be essential for setting the mood of the play. At the very least you must be able to dim or extinguish the house lights in order to define the performance space. This can be done easily enough with a couple of strong overhead lights.

You will not need professional theatrical lighting equipment. Virtually any spotlight-style lamp with an opague reflector will do. In combination with 75-watt floodlight bulbs, a few gooseneck desk lamps can provide very functional if unsepctacular illumination. The overhead light must shed plenty of light on the puppets while shielding the spectators' eyes from the glare of the naked bulbs. Most hardware or household supply stores sell inexpensive clamp lamps with aluminum shades. You can also assemble your own theatrical floodlights by inserting a standard bulb socket in an ordinary coffee can, painted black. If you are feeling inventive, you can improvise clamps or even a full tracking mechanism using bamboo poles or broomsticks suspended from the ceiling (FIG. 7-14).

To light a full marionette stage, you must install a row of floodlights along the bottom of the *proscenium arch*. Proscenium arch is the correct theatrical term for the sheet of plywood that hangs from the top of the two curtain supports. (If you find this grand phrase embarrassing, you can begin referring to it as the "lighting board" as soon as you have installed the floodlight sockets).

Following are instructions for overhead lights.

Materials

- Electrical wire.
- Seven or eight standard light sockets (the type that can be screwed down on a flat surface).
- Dimmer switch.

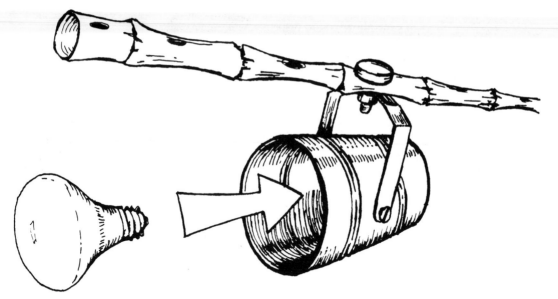

Fig. 7-14. Poles may be used for attaching lighting.

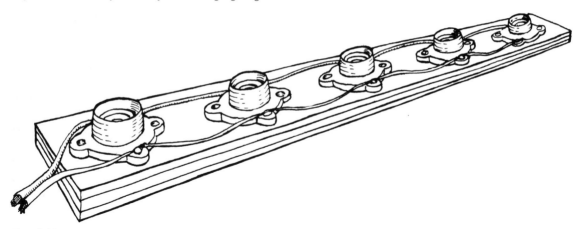

Fig. 7-15. Mount the light sockets along a strip of wood.

1. Mount the light sockets at 7- or 8-inch intervals along a strip of wood or plywood 4 inches wide and 6 feet long (FIG. 7-15).

2. Wire the sockets together, using a fairly heavy gauge of insulated electrical wire. Use "parallel" wiring. A simple way to wire bulbs in parallel is to separate the two insulated strands of the double wire, strip off the insulation at regular intervals along the wire, and wrap the uninsulated segments of the wire around the brass screws on the light sockets (FIG. 7-16).

Note: You might want to install a variety of colored floodlight bulbs that can be controlled independently. This is an excellent way to create special lighting effects. If you want to control the different colors separately, you will have to

152

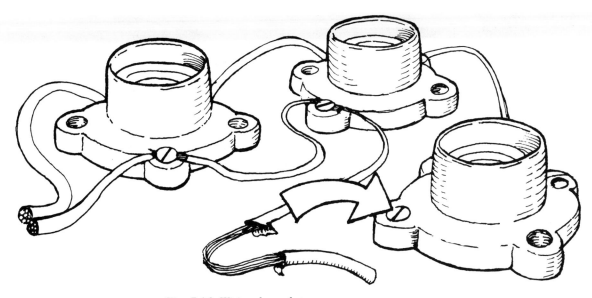

Fig. 7-16. Wiring the sockets.

wire the blues, reds, and whites on separate circuits, and give each circuit its own switch.

3. Attach another strip of wood at right angles to the board on which the light sockets are mounted. This second board will shield the audience from the lights (FIG. 7-17).

4. Hang the completed strip of lights on the bottom lip of the proscenium arch. Attach them at an angle, so that the lights are trained on the lower half of the backdrop. Use metal brackets to attach the strip, bending them to get the angle you want (FIG. 7-18).

5. Fill the empty sockets with 75-watt bulbs and run the whole system through a dimmer switch. It's best to use a genuine theatrical dimmer if you can find one. Ordinary household dimmer switches are quite usable, but they come on too abruptly when you are bringing up the stage lights.

The overhead lights are now finished. To give yourself complete control over the lighting, you might wish to supplement the overhead lights with a row of bulbs down each of the two side panels of the stage. It is also a good idea to install a couple of footlights in front of the stage opening. A pair of standing lamps placed at each front corner of the stage will help to illuminate the downstage area.

STAGE CURTAIN

The stage curtain is a character in the show. It is a very simple character—it can't do much except go up and down. Nevertheless, it is a full character, and one with a strangely commanding presence. When the curtain rises upon a new scene,

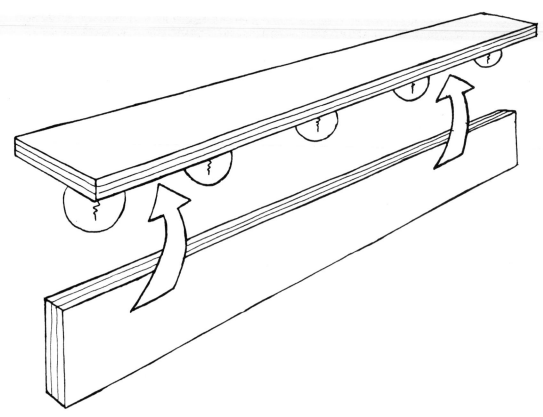

Fig. 7-17. This second board shields the audience from the light.

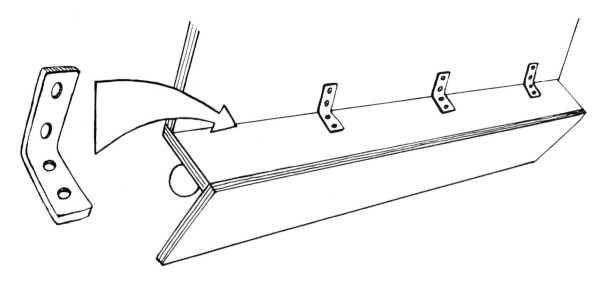

Fig. 7-18. Use brackets to attach the boards of the lighting system.

an expectant hush comes over the audience. When the curtain comes down at the end of the show, the crowd erupts into applause. The stage curtain is a sort of "master of ceremonies" presiding over the transitional moments in the play, which are extremely important. If the play is to win the audience over, such moments must be performed with grace and a touch of ostentation. Therefore, it is essential that your stage curtain be a reliable performer. If it is well and carefully built, it will be a pleasure to use. If it is thrown together in a hurry, it will be an inexhaustible source of embarrassment to you and your troupe.

The simplest kind of curtain is a flat piece of decorative fabric with a wooden rod slipped into the hem at the top and bottom. Ropes are attached to each end of the upper rod. Each rope passes through a pulley attached to hooks at the top of the stage. The ropes are knotted together at one end (FIG. 7-19).

This type of curtain works well, but isn't very exciting to look at. FIGURE 7-20 shows a pleated "Viennese style" curtain that rises in elegant, scalloped folds. The curtain is made out of a loose fabric that won't crease easily. The upper hem of the curtain (folded in pleats) is nailed to a wooden bar. Strings pass through rows of plastic rings sewn to the material of the curtain (these rings are available at sewing supply shops). The strings pass through "pulleys" made out of very large screw eyes. After passing through a screw eye on the far left of the wooden bar, all of the strings are knotted together.

MAKING A SCENE

Scenery is background. That might seem self-evident, but so are all the great truths. The scenic backdrops should keep modestly back, receding behind the puppets and any props that are central to the narrative. If they are too detailed or colorful, they tend to overpower the action of the play. Not that the scenery should be plain: when the curtain comes up on a new scene, the audience should gasp with delight. However, after they have had a chance to admire the view, they should forget about the scenery and turn their undivided attention to the story. The set designer must make this easy for them by not permitting the scenes to upstage the marionettes.

The puppets must be conspicuous against the backgrounds, so the dominant colors of the scenery should contrast with those of the costumes. For the same reason, the scenery should not be too detailed. If the puppet costumes have a lot of pattern on them, be wary of putting patterns into the backgrounds. Also keep in mind that flat, patterned surfaces tend to jump out at the spectator, which can give the setting an oppressive feeling.

Of course, in some circumstances, a congested, chaotic atmosphere will be just what you need. Suppose the protagonist is lost in the woods, or a maze of hallways. You can underscore his lostness by crowding the scene with confusing details. In FIG. 7-21 the patterns of crisscrossed lines help create the illusion of a bustling medieval town, even though there are only two marionettes onstage. In this case the claustrophobic closeness of the buildings is appropriate to the scene.

Notice that the tops of the puppet's heads almost reach the second floors of the houses. If these characters were life-sized, they would be 7 or 8 feet tall,

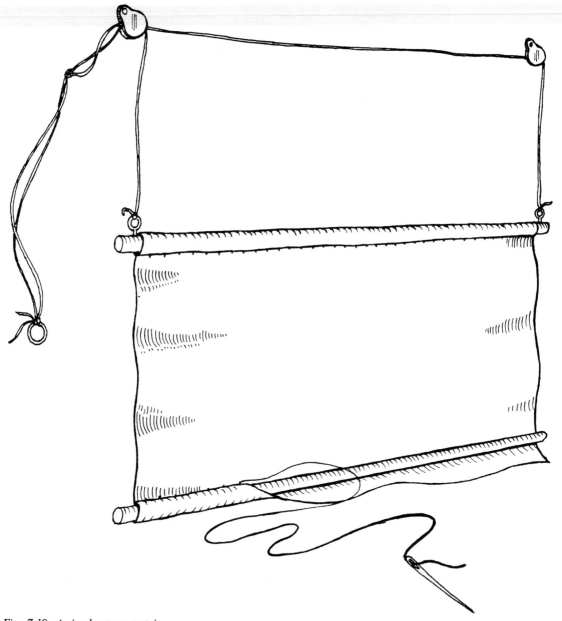

Fig. 7-19. A simple stage curtain.

but here there's nothing particularly disturbing about the picture. When you design your scenes remember that proportions need not be realistic, as long as they are consistent. In fact, if you made everything exactly to scale, the backgrounds would probably look all wrong.

156

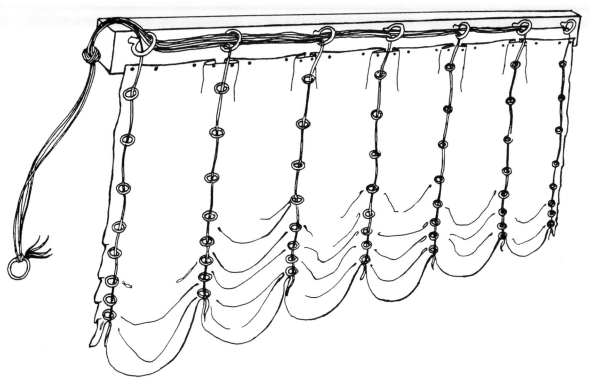

Fig. 7-20. A Viennese style curtain.

Making a scene look crowded is easy. Creating an illusion of depth is much more difficult. To some extent this can be done by careful choice of colors. Deep, intense hues come forward, while pale, hazy colors recede. As a general rule, things that are far away should be rendered in pastel colors, while things that are nearby should be clear and bright. In particular you should use a faint blue for the sky; an intense blue sky will look like the cloth it is painted on.

Another way to create the illusion of depth is by deliberate use of exaggerated perspective. The forest scene in FIG. 7-22 is built on three different levels. Large, leafy boughs made of thin plywood, cut with a jigsaw and realistically painted, are hung from the proscenium arch right at the front of the stage. Further back, two plywood trees are pegged to the stage floor. Finally, a number of trees are painted on the cloth backdrop at the very back of the stage. As they recede, the trees get smaller.

An ambitious set designer can even arrange things so that different levels of scenery interact in full perspective. Getting everything lined up is pretty tricky, but it is well worth the effort for the vivid three-dimensional quality that this technique gives (FIG. 7-23).

The scenery in this illustration is in several parts, which is only a short step from actually building three-dimensional objects on the stage. It can be awkward to incorporate such objects into a show; they take up a lot of room on stage and

Fig. 7-21. A scene in a medieval city.

can be difficult to transport from one auditorium to the next. However, some shows require prominent three-dimensional structures for the puppets to walk through or stand upon. You might want to position one marionette in a tower balcony while another does battle on the stairs below. It wouldn't be difficult to build such a set, provided you don't incorporate any projecting curved surfaces into the design (FIG. 7-24).

Assemble the structure (FIG. 7-25) out of flat pieces of plywood, masonite, or reinforced cardboard, and design it in such a way that the whole thing can be disassembled and packed flat. Use dowel pegs, bolts, wing nuts, Velcro, snap fasteners, hinges, or even masking tape to hold the various parts of the construction together. The entire set piece can be fixed to the stage floor along with any other props that will be used during the scene. Before each performance the structure may be assembled and put to one side behind the stage, where it will remain until it is needed in the show. This scene is then removed and the entire floor, with balcony, staircase, and props attached, can be lifted into place on the stage.

Fig. 7-22. Objects on stage plus painted backdrops give the illusion of depth.

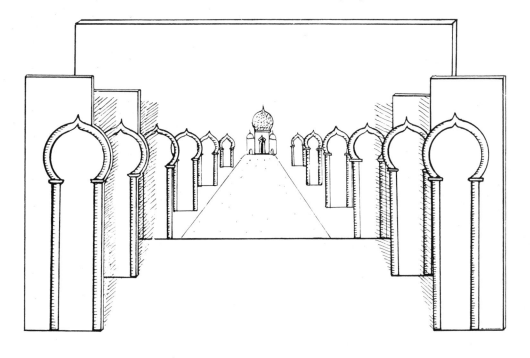

Fig. 7-23. Different levels of scenery allow for a three-dimensional effect.

When designing large set pieces, be sure to leave the puppets plenty of room to maneuver. Make sure that entrances and exits will not be obstructed and that there is sufficient space onstage for all the necessary action to occur. How much room do the puppets need? As much as they can get, and then some. For some reason, no matter how much space there is onstage, you always wish you had more. Remember that, even if the marionette is only 3 inches wide at the shoulders, he might be three times that with his arms stretched out. Therefore, if the puppet is in a tight spot, such as a doorway, he might not be able to do much with his hands.

THE PLAY

What kind of plays can be performed with puppets? Virtually any kind. That's not an exaggeration. Almost every major theatrical form has been successfully adapted for puppets: romantic farce, Greek tragedy, high opera, burlesque, situation comedy, melodrama (FIGS. 7-26 and 7-27). I have even seen a puppet soap opera on daytime television in Quebec. Almost anything that can be done

Fig. 7-24. This scene from Hildegard and the Wolf *shows how foreground scenery can create an illusion of depth. (Photograph by Jano Salinas.)*

with live actors can be done with puppets. I don't mean that it can be done in the same way. On the contrary, puppet theatre is a unique medium and has different requirements. Dramatic techniques that work magnificently with live actors might be unusable or ridiculous with puppets. Dialogue that seems snappy and fast-

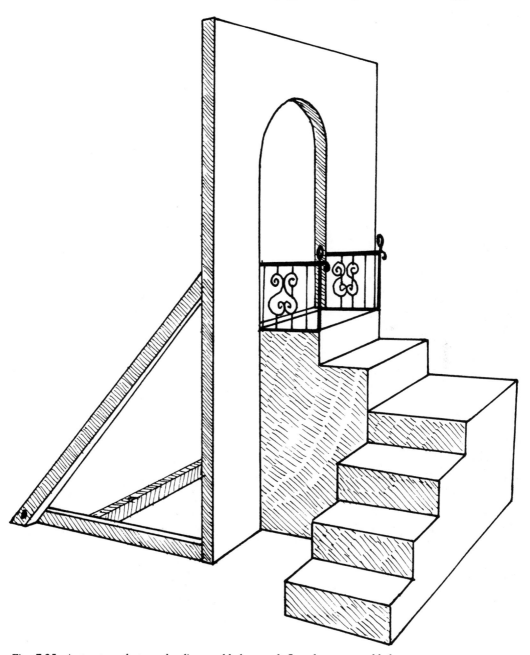

Fig. 7-25. A structure that can be disassembled to pack flat, then reassembled.

paced in the legitimate theatre can be sluggish to the point of catatonia on the puppet stage. So while it is possible to do, say, *King Lear* with puppets, you might find that you'll have to rewrite the play completely.

As you set out to put on a play you have two options. You can write or adapt your own story or you can use a readymade script. Many puppet plays have been published already. The drama section of a well-stocked library should have at least a few volumes containing puppet plays. If you are very lucky, you might find one that is serviceable, but the odds are that none of them will meet your particular needs.

A good marionette play is conceived as much at the visual as at the verbal level, and technical problems are something that no scriptwriter can ignore. A play that is written for one company might require scenery, puppets, and special effects that will not work well on another troupe's stage. If the play was specifically conceived for a large company with a huge operating budget and dozens of actors, it will be extremely difficult to adapt it for a small, mobile stage.

Fig. 7-26. King Minos and his daughter Ariadne, Theseus and the Minotaur, *staged by the Picardi Marionette Theatre. These marionettes were based on ancient Minoan frescoes found in the ruined city of Knossos, Crete. (Photograph by Jano Salinas.)*

Unfortunately, it is not likely that you will find a story you like in a version that is both well written and appropriate for your company. So you will probably want to take the other option: write your own. This gives you the freedom to choose any story you please and stage it in a way that is consistent with your circumstances.

Most marionette companies choose to stage stories that are already well-known to their audience. The main advantage of this is that the puppeteers will have less explaining to do. The audience will be able to follow the narrative no matter how scantily it is sketched out. This is important because, in a puppet show, words must be used sparingly. Dialogue should supply opportunities for action. Puppets should never just stand around conveying information about a story. Remember they are not telling the tale—they are *in* it. All the important events in the story must happen right onstage, in front of the audience. In other words you must not tell a story, you must dramatise it.

Frequently, dramatising means that you must concentrate on the central conflicts in the story, to the exclusion of many other details. It can mean actually falsifying the original tale. If you must, you must. There's no point in being faithful

Fig. 7-27. Ariadne ministers to the wounded Theseus. (Photograph by Jano Salinas.)

to the original story if it makes a tedious puppet show. In fact, if the original narrative contains too little conflict to create dramatic tension, then perhaps you should consider doing another story. Many excellent fairytales make very poor puppet shows because they do not provide opportunities for characters to interact in an interesting way. It is not enough that the characters talk; they must have something to talk *about*. They must have problems to solve, scores to settle, misunderstandings to set straight.

Conflict doesn't have to mean out and out hostility between the puppets (although Punch has had a long and successful career punctuating his off-color jokes with monstrous acts of violence). Conflict can be of a subtler sort. It can consist of one character withholding information from another. It can consist of two characters reacting to a situation in widely divergent ways. In a farce it might hinge entirely on a simple plot device such as a mistaken identity. Whatever the reason, there must be some kind of conflict to propel each scene and provide a motive for dialogue.

Dialogue is not just a way of advancing the bald facts of the story. It is a way of creating and resolving tensions between characters. When you are adapting a story that already exits, you must discover the dramatic possibilities in its characters.

Let's say you are doing the story of *Beauty and the Beast*. In the story told to the brothers Grimm, Beauty's father has no particular characteristics. He is simply an honest man and a loving father. That information is sufficient to make a fine bedtime story, but in a theatrical version of the tale, he will have to be given actions and lines that are completely idiosyncratic and that reveal things about his character. He will have mannerisms, a tone of voice, a way of behaving, and a way of reacting to events. All of this has to be present in the puppet, it has to be present in the way the puppet is manipulated, and above all, it must be present in the script.

Sometimes people are surprised to find out that puppeteers work from a prepared script. It is commonly believed that puppetry is an improvisatory, "oral" form of theatre. It is true that puppeteers are as free to improvise as any actor, but if anything, puppetry is more controlled and disciplined than ordinary theatre—because the technical, logistical problems involved in mounting a puppet production are usually far greater. This is particularly true of string puppetry, where everything that happens onstage must be planned out in the greatest detail. An impromptu line or gesture might result in snarled strings, tricks that fizzle, or sound effects that come too late. The difficulty of coordinating all these movements makes it essential that you work from a set script, and that script will eventually have to be written down.

It might not be necessary, however, to write down the script before the first rehearsal. If you are not pressed for time, you might wish to develop a script by improvisation. Developing a script can be a group effort. Each member of the cast can make up his or her own lines, experimenting with different approaches to the scene. Ideas will occur to you as you work, and you can try them out immediately. This can be a pleasant way to spend your Sunday afternoons, while providing a means for nonwriters to "nonwrite" their own play. If you are intimidated by the prospect of writing a show—even a puppet show—this way of working may be for you. In any case it will be a lot easier than staring at a blank pad of foolscap, struggling to drag the whole show out of your imagination.

Improvising a show will work best if there is a "director" watching each scene to determine which lines work and which don't. After you have established a formula that works, you can commit the whole show to paper and give everyone in the cast a copy. After that, you can make changes as they occur to you and note them in the margins of the written text.

VIII

Special Effects

And now, directed by a hand unseen
The finished puppet struts before the scene,
Exalts a treble voice and eunuch tone
And squeaks his part in accents not his own.

"A Puppet Show" (1716)
Joseph Addison

Everything that happens on a marionette stage is a special effect simply because everything has to be done with strings. Imagine living your daily life without touching anything directly, doing everything with threads and wires. Picking up your toothbrush would become a delicate and time-consuming operation. Combing your hair would be a major undertaking, requiring an elaborate system of pulleys, nooses, and counterweights. Fixing a cup of coffee would be a towering feat of domestic engineering. You would be lucky if you managed to finish breakfast by the end of the day (and I can't imagine how you would scrub the frying pan afterwards). The exercise would produce more comedy than coffee, but it would also provide an excellent introduction the art of string puppetry.

The fact is, puppets are enormously inefficient. That's one of the things people like about them. Almost everyone finds it pleasurable to see ordinary things done preposterously. Watching a person drink a glass of water is not too exciting. As entertainment, it is definitely a last resort. But watching a person drink a whole glass of water while reciting the oath of allegiance—that's actually quite amusing, at least the first time you see it done. Puppets can be amusing in much the same way.

I don't want to give the wrong impression. People are intrigued by the roundabout way in which puppets must do things, but you can't build a show around that. A show that is nothing but one trick after another will start to wear thin after only a few minutes, and somewhere between the toothbrush and the coffee, the audience will completely lose interest. The love of ingenuity for its own sake, which can lead a person to build a ship in a bottle or write the Lord's Prayer 200 times on the back of a postage stamp, has no place in the puppet theatre.

Still, occasions will arise when you will have to figure out a way of making the puppets (or the scenery) do something unusual. We might call these *special* special effects, to distinguish them from the ordinary feats of magic that puppets perform as a matter of course. In a typical marionette show, nearly every scene will call for at least one unique device or effect. Consequently, you as the puppeteer must also be an inventor. You will have to invent simple mechanisms, such as a way of getting the puppet to take off his hat. And you will have to invent large scenic effects: a tropical storm, a disappearing castle, a volcanic eruption.

As you plan your show in advance, some of these things might strike you as nearly impossible—but don't be discouraged. The more impossible the concept sounds, the more impressive the final result will be. And impressive effects are not necessarily complicated or hard to create. Often the audience will be transfixed by what might seem to you the most crude and simple tricks. In fact, people are often more powerfully struck by the boldness of an effect than by its realism.

The important thing is to cultivate an audacious attitude. The puppet world is small—so think big. A puppeteer should have no sense of proportion. Abandon common sense; throw practicality to the winds. There are virtually no limits to the effects you can create.

Let's take an example, something ambitious. Suppose you are doing a marionette version of Cecil B. De Mille's well-known movie epic *The Ten Commandments*. (I'd like to see the Royal Shakespeare Company attempt that!) First you must assemble your cast of thousands. The movie version gives us magnificent desert panoramas, teeming with dispossessed Israelites and cohorts of Egyptian soldiers marching to their doom. You already know you can't have thousands of puppeteers milling about backstage, so how can you recreate those scenes? To start with, you should be able to cut a few corners.

A relatively small number of marionettes will make your tiny stage look very busy indeed, so you can probably dispense with the thousands and make do with a cast of dozens. However, even that is too many marionettes for three or four puppeteers to manipulate. The solution? You will have to string several puppets on each control. Better still, why not put all the puppets on one control so that a single puppeteer can move them about? Build them in a clump so that all the puppet's bodies are stuck together (FIG. 8-1). Because the puppets in the front of the crowd will hide the ones in the middle and back, there is no need to build separate bodies for them. Just attach the various heads and limbs to a cloth bag or panel of wood and string the whole thing to one control. The heads and hands

Fig. 8-1. One puppeteer can manipulate a dozen marionettes if they are all attached together.

Fig. 8-2. A crowd painted on Masonite panels.

might be strung together to a single moveable crosspiece on the marionette control, so that the puppeteers can lift all the heads and arms at the same time.

Perhaps you had your heart set on a bigger crowd. Very well. Paint as many faces as you want on panels of masonite or thin plywood. Mount several of the panels on the stage and move them back and forth from the wings. Each panel should be somewhat lower than the one behind it so that the audience can see all the faces (FIG. 8-2).

The same technique can be used to make waves on an ocean—which might be useful when it comes time to part the Red Sea! If you are not satisfied with these ideas, there are plenty of other ways to raise a crowd. How about mounting a row of puppets on springs so that they sway and bounce when they are pushed? How about painting the crowd on transparent sheets of acetate and casting the image with an overhead projector? There are all sorts of possibilities.

STRING TRICKS: MANIPULATING OBJECTS

A special arrangement of strings that permits the puppet to pick a flower or throw a ball might prevent him from doing anything else. You should look on each string as a potential tangle, and avoid tying your puppets down with specialized strings. Sometimes there is a more straightforward way to do the things you have to do, or sometimes you might not have to do those things at all.

Perhaps the most common problem is making the puppets manipulate objects. This is something that does not come naturally to marionettes. Hand puppets do it well, because their arms contain human fingers. But lifting, carrying, and transferring objects with marionettes might involve a bit of planning.

Some objects are easier to move than others. If you can fit the puppet's hand under the handle of a basket or bucket, then you can probably heft it around without

Fig. 8-3. Some objects are easy to move.

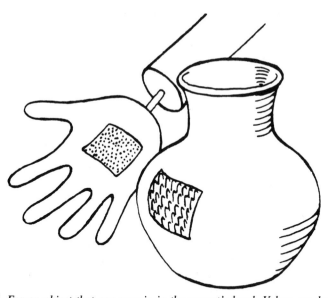

Fig. 8-4. For an object that can remain in the puppet's hand, Velcro can be used.

the help of additional strings. You can control the object by working the puppet's hand string (FIG. 8-3).

If the puppet does not have to let go of the object he picks up, you can place a hook or a patch of Velcro on the palm of the hand (FIG. 8-4). If you use Velcro, make sure to place the soft side—the one without the little plastic hooks—on the hand. The hooked side will tend to snag strings and cling to fibrous surfaces.

A more reliable way to do the same thing is to attach a thread to the object, as if it were a puppet itself. The marionette catches the thread between his fingers while the puppeteer pulls the object up toward the hand. When the puppeteer wants to set the object down, he has only to release the string. This technique is unlikely to end in a tangle (FIG. 8-5).

If you want the object to seem to come to the puppet's hand of its own accord, you might wish to pass the object's string through the palm of the hand, as in FIG. 8-6. For this method to work, everything must be arranged before the scene begins. Throughout the scene, up until the moment when the puppet actually seizes the object, the puppeteer must be careful not to jostle the string so that the object

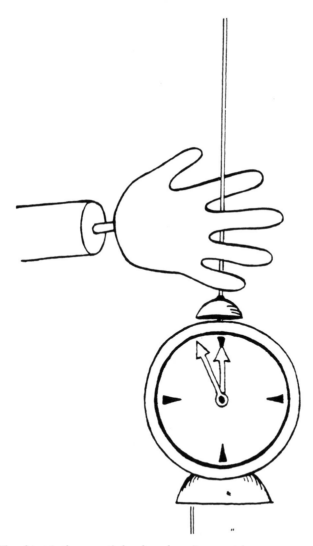

Fig. 8-5. The object in the puppet's hand can have its own string.

172

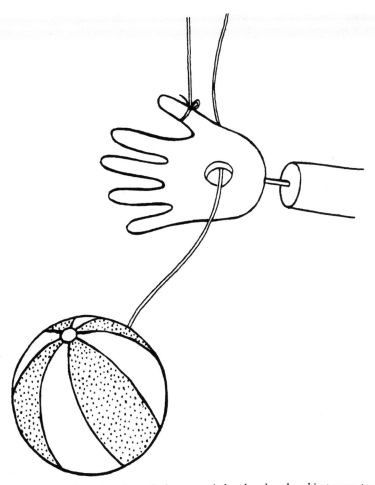

Fig. 8-6. Passing the string through the puppet's hand makes the object seem to come to the puppet.

moves prematurely. Needless to say, this restricts the marionette's mobility a great deal.

Transferring an object from one puppet to another is difficult to do using strings alone. The easiest way to accomplish a transfer is to pick the object up with a long hook of slender wire. One puppeteer manipulates the object with the wire hook, while the other puppeteers make their marionettes behave as if they are lifting and carrying it (FIG. 8-7).

Sometimes you will find it useful to draw the puppet's hand to something, usually a part of his body. If the puppet has to put his hands over his eyes for example, or bring a bottle to his lips, you can run a string right through his head. In FIG. 8-8 you can see that pulling the string (A) will draw the hand automatically to the place where the string emerges. Note that this is an extra string, and to control the hand in the usual way you will have to include an ordinary hand string (B) as well.

173

Fig. 8-7. Use a slender wire to transfer objects from one puppet to another.

A similar technique is used to make the puppet remove his hat (FIG. 8-9). Run the special hand string through the brim of his hat. The hat has two guiding strings that serve as runners, ensuring that hat and hand will always travel straight up and down. When you pull on the hand string, the hand comes directly to the hat and then takes the hat off the head in one smooth motion.

By now you can probably see how most of these string tricks work. In almost every case there is a "guiding" string and a "pulling" string. Sometimes, as in the case of the horn blower in FIG. 8-8, the pulling string itself can double as the guiding string. Most string tricks are just extensions of these same principles. FIGURE 8-10 shows a bird flying from his cage to a tree branch. But you can adapt the basic method to make two puppets throw a ball back and forth, or to make an airplane fly across the sky.

Some objects must be manipulated in a particularly complex way. These require a more elaborate stringing. FIGURE 8-11 shows a marionette who can play the violin. He walks onstage with the fiddle in one hand and bow in the other, his two arms dangling at either side of his body. He bows deeply, then draws the violin to his chin and begins to play. This is accomplished by means of an extremely clever arrangement of strings. It is not known who invented this technique, but it was first described in detail by the puppeteer, author H.W. Whanslaw, in 1939.

The marionette is attached to a vertical control. Notice in FIG. 8-11 the pivoting metal rod (e) on the vertical crosspiece of the control. This can be made

Fig. 8-8. This action is accomplished by running a string through the puppet's head.

Fig. 8-9. This puppet can tip his hat when the puppeteer moves the hand.

Fig. 8-10. A bird can fly to his cage by means of a special stringing arrangement.

of bent coat hanger, passed through a hole drilled in the dowelling of the control. When the bent rod is pivoted upwards, the violin string (d) comes automatically to the screw eye on the puppet's chin (f), while it simultaneously pulls the bow toward the screw eye at the bridge of the violin (g). The hand and bow are operated by means of two strings (a and b) attached to a removable crosspiece. Note that the bow-string (the part of the bow that would be made of horse hairs on a real violin) is attached to string (d) by a ring. The ring permits the bow to slide back and forth while it is held close to the bridge of the violin (g). If you find these explanations confusing, study the diagram. It is actually not too complicated, once you know what is going on.

Any puppet can play the violin, provided he is strung up correctly. But once the strings are on, he must remain attached to his violin throughout the scene. This makes him a specialist, like the stunt puppets of Chapter VI. I recommend that you use such specialized stringing as little as possible. Stick to tricks that don't limit the puppet in any way. There are some very good ones.

Take this spaghetti-eater as an example of such a puppet. When she has finished her meal she can get up and walk away from the table, completely unencumbered. A puppeteer hidden offstage draws the "spaghetti" (made of bootlaces) through a hole in the puppet's head. The puppet must be seated with the back of its head toward the backcloth. The spaghetti is drawn through a slit in the cloth, and the audience never sees where it goes (FIG. 8-12).

TRICKS WITH PROPS

A prop is any object onstage that is neither a character nor a piece of scenery. Some props do nothing but add to the atmosphere of a scene, others are essential to the plot. The magical lamp in the story of Aladdin is a prop of the latter kind,

Fig. 8-11. A violin player requires elaborate stringing.

Fig. 8-12. This puppet can eat spaghetti.

an inanimate object that is as important to the story as any of the characters. Often this kind of prop has to do something special. Obviously there's no way I can foresee all the kinds of props you will need and the tricks they will perform. However, you will not find it difficult to improvise mechanical illusions that work.

Sometimes the simplest tricks are the most effective. "Talking boxes" are a good example. These treasure chests are heaped full of gold, silver, and precious gems—or, if you are on a budget, gold-painted gravel, silvery brocade, green sequins, and red plastic beads. As the puppet approaches, the chest lids open and close like mouths, while an alluring voice beckons to her from within the hoard (FIG. 8-13). This "trick"—a single string attached to a hinged lid—could scarcely

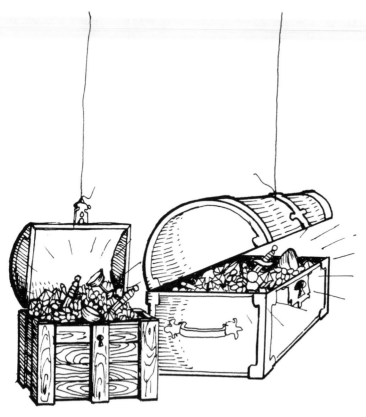

Fig. 8-13. Strings allow these to be "talking" boxes.

be less ingenious. It works because it is simple and dramatic. Such devices are the mainstay of puppet magic.

Often, the element of surprise is what makes a simple trick succeed. The principle of the jack-in-the-box can be used to good effect to make a vampire-in-the-coffin, or four and twenty blackbirds in a pie (FIG. 8-14).

When things suddenly appear or disappear, the audience will reward your ingenuity with an appreciative gasp. People delight in sudden disclosures, as every stage magician knows. Magic is a sort of peek-a-boo for all ages. "Now you see it, now you don't:" in one way or another, this is the key to every conjuror's routine, whether he is pulling a rabbit from a hat, or making an elephant disappear.

Puppet conjuring relies on the same universal love of sudden reversals. Take for instance the case of the disappearing banquet. The gluttonous marionette sits down to a magnificent feast of plaster apples and papier-mâché ham. As she reaches out for the ham—ping!—it disappears. She pauses, startled, then reaches for another dish. It too vanishes. Spying a turkey leg, she rises from her chair and stalks toward the plate, determined that this one will not evade her. With a triumphant shout she pounces upon the drumstick, but it is snatched away. One after the other, the plates vanish. Finally, she flies into a rage and lunges for

Fig. 8-14. Four and twenty blackbirds appear in a pie.

the table, intending to smash it into kindling. But the table itself disappears in a magnificent puff of smoke, and the scene degenerates into a slapstick chase as the glutton makes as if to steal the dog's bone.

The disappearing banquet has to be set up carefully before the scene begins. The table is actually a small box with several holes in the top surface, large enough for the plates of food to pass through. Several screw eyes are mounted at the bottom of the box. Rubber bands are stretched between the screw eyes and small hooks on the papier-mâché food. The plates rest above the hole, supported by pieces of rigid wire bent into crescent shapes (coat-hanger wire will work well). Long threads are attached to the U-shaped wires so that they may be pulled away by puppeteers standing in the wings. When the wire is pulled out from under the food, the elastic bands pull the plates down through the holes in the table

181

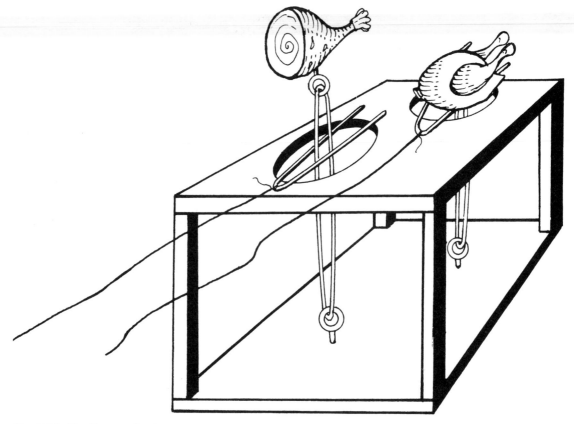

Fig. 8-15. The disappearing banquet.

top. It all happens so quickly that nobody can really see what is happening (FIG. 8-15).

The holes in the table may be concealed beneath a patterned tablecloth. Cut a slit into the cloth where the food will rest. (If the cloth has a pattern of stripes the slits will not be too visible). The U-shaped hooks should be hidden *under* the table cloth, between the plates and the top surface of the box. Obviously you will have to make sure that there is room under the cloth for each wire to be removed without obstruction (FIG. 8-16). Later in this chapter, I'll describe a technique for making the whole table disappear in a puff of smoke.

Often you will need to transform your props in some way. You might want something to grow gradually larger or longer, for instance. In the story *Sleeping Beauty*, a tall thicket of brambles grows around Beauty's castle as the enchantment settles upon her. For a puppet version of the popular tale, you might want the thorns to sprout right in front of the audience.

The stems of the plants that will be sprouting should be made of soft cord, dyed a convincing shade of green. The leaves and blossoms can be cut from pieces of supple cloth and sewn to the cord. Each plant is simply coiled up under a papier-

182

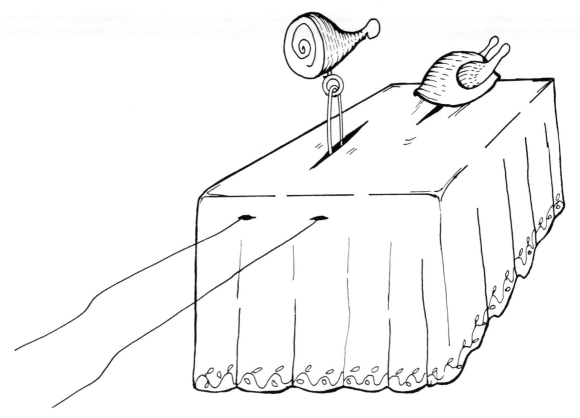

Fig. 8-16. The mechanics of the disappearing banquet.

mâché embankment on the stage or under a hole in the stage floor. A piece of cloth with a slit in it is placed over the mouth of the bank or hole and a string is attached to the top of the plant. To make the flower ''grow'' the puppeteer simply draws the plant out through the slit in the cloth. The bushier the plant, the more miraculous the effect will seem (FIG. 8-17).

SMOKE AND FIRE

There's nothing like a clash of cymbals, a flash of lightning, and a good puff of smoke to announce the arrival of a wizard or the transformation of a hedgehog into a marriageable prince. The lightning flash is as easy as flicking a switch, and the cymbals speak for themselves—but how can you make a convincing cloud of smoke?

The answer, as usual, depends on your precise needs. If the smoke must appear suddenly you should probably use a commercially produced flash powder. It is possible to mix your own flash powders and smoke bombs, but I strongly recommend that you buy a premixed formula from a magic shop or theatrical supply outlet. These are not only easier to use, but much safer and possibly more reliable as well.

Fig. 8-17. Flowers can appear as if by magic.

You might find that different commercial smoke powders have different properties. Some make a lot of smoke and others are all flash. The most useful blends produce a bright flash and a thick column of smoke. There are several ways of igniting the powder. In some cases you can simply drop a lit match into a pan containing a quantity of flash formula. This is possible when the source of the fire is hidden, so that the hand holding the match cannot be seen from the audience. This might be a good way to make a volcano.

184

When attempting a volcano, make sure to leave a hollow space in the back so you will be able to introduce your hand from the rear without the audience seeing it. When you light the powder, smoke will emerge from the chimney of the volcanic cone. "Lava," made from strips of soft, red cloth, may be pulled from the crater with strings. You can also place the pan of smoke powder below the stage floor. Station your smallest puppeteer under the stage to light the powder at the appropriate moment. The smoke will rise through a grate.

Another way to make smoke is to tip a quantity of flash powder onto an electrical hot plate. The hot plate may be mounted on or under the stage floor, depending on the configuration of your scenery (FIG. 8-18). *Caution:* If you select this method you must take certain precautions. Nothing flammable must come anywhere near the hot plate. Because practically everything in a puppet show is flammable, you must be extremely careful. Surround the hot plate with a nonflammable insulating material, such as the flame-resistant panels that are used behind wood stoves.

It is possible to ignite smoke powder with electricity. This method permits you to conceal the small dish of powder anywhere on stage. You can activate the flash from behind the scenes, simply by flicking a switch. The mechanism is not hard to build, but learning to use it will require practice.

To build the mechanism, you will need: two short nails, a piece of ceramic tile, a small tin can, a length of electrical wire, a switch and a standard plug.

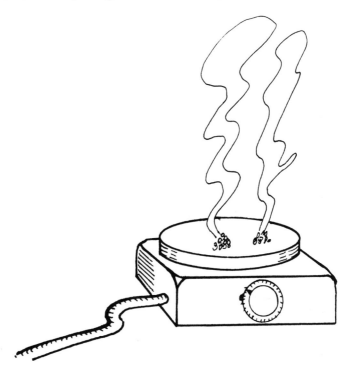

Fig. 8-18. Smoke can be made using an electrical hot plate.

Find a small piece of flat ceramic tile (glass will also work quite well) and glue it into the bottom of a shallow metal dish. A small tuna or salmon can is about the right size. Use epoxy to attach the title to the metal; no other glue will hold. You might have to break the tile to fit into the can. It doesn't matter if the tile is irregularly shaped: its only purpose is to insulate the bottom of the can. Glue two nails to the tile, about 1½ inches apart, as in FIG. 8-19.

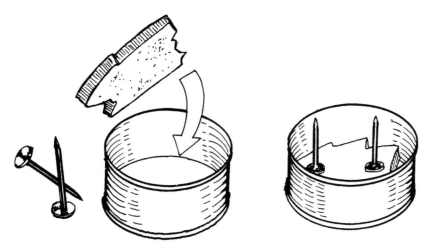

Fig. 8-19. To ignite smoke powder using electricity, you can use a mechanism like this one.

Select a piece of double, insulated stranded copper wire—the kind that is used on lamps and household appliances—and fit it with a plug and switch (FIG. 8-20). Strip ½ inch of insulation from the free end of the wire, and attach to each of the two nails. Wrap the stranded copper tightly around the base of each nail and, if possible, solder it in place.

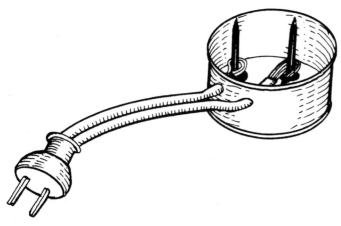

Fig. 8-20. Fitting the wire with a plug and switch.

Before using this flash mechanism you must make a sort of "fuse." Remove three or four *individual* strands from a length of stranded copper wire. Wrap these between the two nails (FIG. 8-21). If you know anything about electricity (and you should not attempt this unless you do), you know that this will create a potential short circuit.

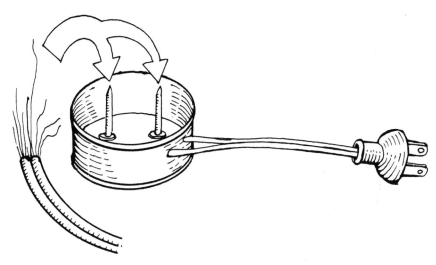

Fig. 8-21. Making the fuse.

Now you must heap flash powder around the nails and the exposed copper wires. When the mechanism is plugged into an electrical socket and switched on, the electricity will surge through the exposed strands of copper wire, causing them to become extremely hot. They will melt and break apart, exactly like the lead connector in a glass fuse, and as they do so they will ignite the flash powder. Note: If there are not enough strands of copper wire running between the two nails, then there is a possibility that the powder will not catch fire. If you use too many strands you will blow a fuse. *Caution:* Children should not attempt this trick.

A puff of smoke can be used to distract the audience while you make puppets or large objects vanish. Everything must be precisely timed and coordinated for this trick to work. First, create some suspense. This is important: If you don't build up to the trick gradually, you will squander half the effect.

Let's say you are transforming a prince into a toad. The witch mutters her incantation, dances an evil jig, waves her magic soup ladle and . . . nothing happens. The prince laughs. Quaking with rage, she tries again. Again, nothing happens. On her third try there is a puff of smoke, and a loud crash. The scene goes dark for one brief second, and the prince vanishes. In his place there is a huge fat toad. A melancholy violin begins to play as the smoke clears, and the prince hops away, croaking mournfully.

It takes several puppeteers to accomplish a transformation like this. One puppeteer manipulates the prince while another stands ready with a toad puppet.

A third puppeteer manipulates the witch and a fourth operates the lights. At the moment of the transformation, the fourth puppeteer flicks off all the stage lights and trips the electrical switch that ignites the smoke powder. The puppeteer who is holding the prince plucks him up by his strings and lifts him over the backcloth. At the same moment the toad puppet is dropped into the prince's place. The flash powder distracts the audience and provides a smoke screen. The darkness and smoke hide the prince as he is lifted out of the scene and the toad drops from the sky. If possible, a fifth puppeteer hits a gong, drum, or cymbal (the puppeteer who operates the lights might be able to manage this).

Obviously you will have to rehearse this trick a number of times before it will work smoothly. With practice you'll find it's possible to complete the transformation so quickly that nobody will guess how the trick is done.

Smoke powder is fine for sudden puffs, but too much of it will asphyxiate your audience. If you want a continuous stream of smoke, you are better off using dry ice. A small block of dry ice dropped into a pan of warm water creates clouds of cool, white vapor. This is perfect for seething vats, bubbling cauldrons, and the Hudson river. The vapor is heavier than air, so it can be used to create a "misty graveyard" effect. Unfortunately, dry ice is hard to procure and cannot be stored for long periods of time. Somebody will have to purchase a block of it before each performance.

While we are on the subject of smoke, I should point out that there is a traditional technique for making smoke seem to emerge from inside a puppet. This trick adds realism to any mythical beast, but it is especially useful for dragons. The dragon must be built with two tubes running from his back, up his neck, down his snout, and up his nostrils. Unfortunately, making the dragon puff smoke requires that the puppeteer breathe fire. The courageous puppeteer must be prepared to suck in the smoke of a lit cigarette and exhale into the tubes. The tubes, which can be cut from a rubber skipping rope, pass unobtrusively through a slit in the backcloth (FIG. 8-22).

The dragon trick can also be used to a make a "smoker" puppet. Simply run the tubes through the puppet's head to his nostrils.

MAKING FIRE

You might think fire would be one of the most difficult special effects. It is not. However, it is one of the most impressive. This effect is so good that I have given it a heading all to itself.

A convincing fire must (a) give off light, (b) flicker, and (c) crackle. In my method, the light is supplied by a light bulb, the flicker is supplied by an electric fan, and the crackle is supplied by strips of orange cellophane.

First, buy a roll of flimsy orange cellophane. This must be a relatively "brittle" material—you cannot use the kind of plastic wrap that is used for preserving foods. Stationery and art supply stores sometimes sell lightweight plastics, used for making decorations and for covering books. If you cannot find a pale orange, buy clear cellophane and tint it. You can paint on cellophane and acetate with special translucent paints, available at art supply stores.

Fig. 8-22. A fire-breathing dragon.

Cut the plastic into narrow blades, 8 to 10 inches long, and tape along the edge of a stick. Mount a floodlight bulb and an electric fan out of sight underneath the place where the fire is to occur. Rest the stick of cellophane ''fire'' on a screen or grate (FIG. 8-23). When the fan is switched on, the fire will leap into life. The light from the bulb will be refracted through the flickering cellophane, making it seem as if the fire is emitting its own light. When the lights are out it looks and sounds exactly like real fire.

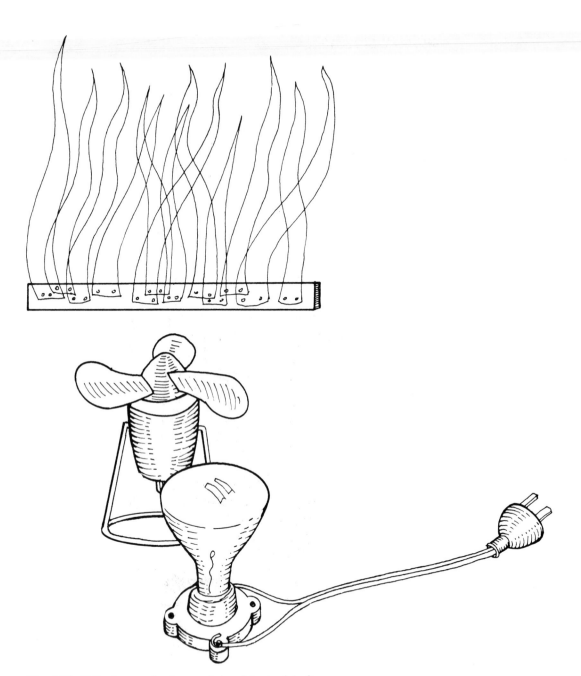

Fig. 8-23. Cellophane and a fan can be used to simulate fire.

If you can't acquire the appropriate kind of cellophane, you can do the same trick with strips of very fine silk. The silk will not crackle like fire, but you can create the appropriate sound effects simply by crumpling sheets of paper behind the scenes.

SHADOW EFFECTS

Shadow puppet shows are popular throughout the Far East, and have been for thousands of years. In these spectacles the puppeteers sit on the opposite side of a cloth screen, which is lit from behind by a torch or electric light. The puppeteers manipulate flat cutout figures, which the spectators on the other side of the screen see as moving silhouettes (FIG. 8-24).

There is a Chinese story about how the art had its start. The emperor Wu-ti is said to have been so grieved by the death of his wife Wang that he lost all interest in living. The nobles of his court did all they could to alleviate his suffering,

Fig. 8-24. The silhouette of a Javanese-style shadow puppet.

but he would not be consoled. One day a mysterious traveler showed up at the emperor's palace, claiming he could call forth the dead woman's spirit. Sciao-wong, as the traveler was called, stretched a piece of cloth over a doorway and sat the emperor before it. He made the emperor promise not to interfere with the cloth screen, and then proceeded to make Wang's ghost appear behind it. As the story goes, the emperor became so emotional at the sight of his late wife that he leapt up, and ripped way the cloth. Behind the screen was Sciao-wong, holding a flat shadow figure in front of a torch. Thus began the art of the shadow puppet; and thus ended the career of Sciao-wong: Wu-ti flew into a rage at the insolence of the deception, and had the poor showman's head chopped off.

Taking our inspiration from the oriental shadow theatre, we can produce a number of remarkable effects. Shadow figures can be combined with ordinary marionettes to establish different levels of a narrative. For example, a dream sequence or a story-within-the-story might be projected on the backdrop behind the puppets.

Position a strong light behind a plain cotton backcloth and extinguish all other stage lights. Cut the shadow figures out of cardboard or thin plywood and mount them on sticks of ¼-inch dowelling (FIG. 8-25). You will find that pressing the figures against the screen gives a sharp, clear silhouette, and that pulling them away from the cloth, toward the light, causes the outlines to blur and the shapes to grow larger.

Shadow figures don't have to be black silhouettes. Make parts of the shapes out of colored, transparent acetate. The colors will shine through the cotton screen like stained glass.

By an extension of this device, you can create instant changes of scenery and cause fabulous shapes to appear as if by magic. Let's say you want to make a desert landscape burst into bloom. First, make a backcloth showing rolling sand dunes and a pale desert sky. Use cloth dyes to color the sky and sand; paint tends to make the cloth opague. You can probably get away with using an oil-based paint if you thin it down so that it stains the cloth rather than coating it.

Buy a sheet of clear acetate, about ¹⁄₁₆-inch thick and as large as the backcloth of your stage. Paint a lush tropical scene on the plastic sheet, using special acetate paints, which are available at art supply stores. Hang the acetate behind the backcloth on the stage as in FIG. 8-26. Place a strong light backstage behind the acetate. When it is time for the desert to bloom, dim the stage lights and gradually bring up the other light. The desert will fade out of sight, and in its place there will be a paradisal garden, shimmering peacefully.

Fig. 8-25. A shadow figure.

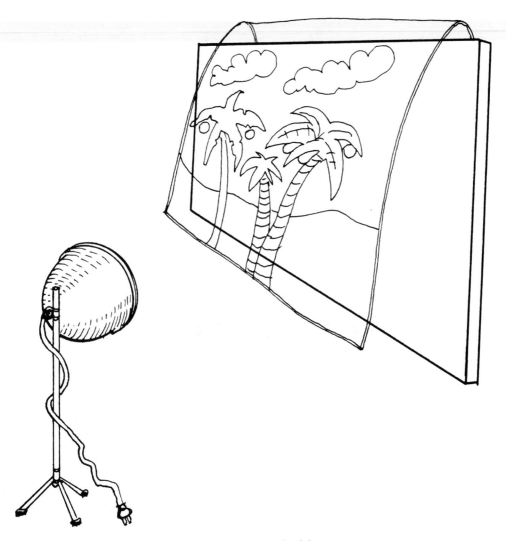

Fig. 8-26. Special effects can be created using acetate backdrops.

INDEX

Edited by Cherie R. Blazer